THE GOLDEN AGE
OF STREAMLINING

COLIN ALEXANDER

AMBERLEY

Acknowledgements

I would like to thank my godfather, Bob Kelley, for his assistance in preparing this book, as well as all of the photographic contributors.

First published 2021

Amberley Publishing
The Hill, Stroud,
Gloucestershire, GL5 4EP

www.amberley-books.com

ISBN: 978 1 4456 9334 7 (print)
ISBN: 978 1 4456 9335 4 (ebook)

British Library Cataloguing in Publication Data.
A catalogue record for this book is available from the British Library.

Typesetting by SJmagic DESIGN SERVICES, India.
Printed in Great Britain.

Contents

Foreword

Streamlining can make any kind of moving machine look good. It can sometimes increase the performance of that machine, and occasionally make it worse. What can be forgotten is that streamlining can be equally beneficial or detrimental when applied inside the machine. In the days of my youth, motorcycles were my way of life. The racing types would write into the magazines on the secrets of tuning the engine. High lift cams, lighter pistons, you name it, but inevitably it came down to the basic hard work of polishing the inside of your engine and improving gas flow into and out of the cylinder by filing off bits of the induction and exhaust tracts in order to speed and increase the respective flow of gases. More power, see! That was then, but manufacturers are still at it, without using the internal aerodynamics of engines as a sales pitch. External aerodynamics still sells, cars in particular. My own current car has a drag coefficient of 0.24 – better than most. That's part of the sales pitch, and it may be a good thing. I just liked the look of the car.

I digress, just a bit. Many years ago, my first job out of college was a Technical Assistant with the firm of CA Parsons in Newcastle. Parsons' Heaton Works made steam turbines for power stations. These were very large machines, and looking good was not part of the design brief. It was the internal aerodynamics that mattered in terms of their operating efficiency. So my job was largely measuring losses on turbine blade shapes in a wind tunnel. What was involved was measuring pressures close to the blade shape using a pitot tube (a device for measuring flow velocity) and finding out from that where vortices were thrown off the blade. Vortices mean losses in energy transfer within the machine. Visual modelling was done in the wind tunnel using smoke, the kind they use in theatrical and musical performances now, and sometimes by observing the effects of different blade settings by painting a large blade with a colourant in a light oil painted or sprayed on to the enlarged blade shape. Messy and not very elegant but it looked good in reports. My work involved sonic airflow. Another section and an adjacent wind tunnel handled supersonic airflow. Tips of larger blades on the low-pressure stage turbine could easily travel at supersonic speeds, giving differences in fluid flow characteristics.

The department I worked in, the Research Department, was housed in one big office, crammed desk to desk, with three offices at one end for managers/big-shot scientists.

Near my desk, at the opposite end, was an annexe for the draughtsmen. One wall of this annexe was given over to files, ancient and modern. If you went to the top shelf, left-hand corner of the open shelves, you could pull out a file of notes which had been opened by Charlie Parsons himself, I would guess in around the 1880s. Sir Charles Algernon Parsons was one of these genius engineers the Victorian era produced. He was the inventor of the reaction steam turbine, on which the business was built, although he worked on many other concepts. He was, apparently, a keen fisherman, and used the beautifully streamlined shape of the trout as a model for his turbine blades. These notes provided a design concept for a water tunnel, used to develop the shape of turbine blade sections. If you can imagine the trout shape being bent into various angles, you could see his original ideas forming. An open-topped water tunnel was constructed, and a variety of wooden blade shapes were tested with a number of different blade pitches and water flows. The vortices from blades could be seen by the disturbance of the water around the blade shapes, and the internal effects of the pitch, the gap between adjacent blades. His original turbines were constructed based on results from these early tests. I think that the best example of streamlining inside and out would be his steam yacht *Turbinia*, which had an incredibly beautiful hull shape and hidden streamlining in his turbine blade shapes and settings.

I hope that Sir Charles Parsons' original notes went to a science museum, for nothing now remains of Parsons' Heaton Works.

Bob Kelley

1

The Golden Age of Streamlining

That a book about the glamorous, high-speed era of streamlining should begin with the internal workings of stationary steam turbines may seem surprising. Legendary locomotive engineer Sir Nigel Gresley would appreciate it, though, for he ensured that his trademark external streamlining was made truly effective by similar treatment inside his machines, about which there will be more later.

The firm of Parsons is very close to my heart, for it is where my late father 'served his time', and Bob Kelley, who contributed the foreword to this book, was my dad's best friend.

Sir Charles Parsons' work on his steam yacht *Turbinia* bore fruit when she spectacularly gatecrashed the Royal Navy's Spithead review, leading to a revolution in maritime propulsion. *Turbinia* can be admired today in Newcastle's excellent Discovery Museum, and she epitomises that combination of external and internal streamlining.

The design aesthetic of products in the Edwardian era and the early years of the reign of George V was firmly rooted in the Victorian era. Motor vehicles were little more than

Sir Charles Parsons' experimental steam yacht *Turbinia* on permanent display inside Discovery Museum in Newcastle. Her slender streamlined hull and internally streamlined turbines made her the fastest thing on the waves in 1894. (Colin Alexander)

horseless carriages, railway locomotives were enlarged versions of their nineteenth-century ancestors, and furniture was very staid and traditional. Everything was dark and very upright in appearance.

This aesthetic continued into the early interwar years after 1918. This was, for many, a time of great hardship. The world was recovering from the ravages of the First World War, during an era characterised by the Spanish Flu pandemic, the General Strike, the Wall Street Crash and the subsequent Great Depression.

In 1917, while Russia was in the throes of the Bolshevik uprising, a quieter kind of revolution began in the Netherlands, establishing a brave new direction in architecture and interior design. This was De Stijl, to be followed two years later by Germany's Bauhaus school of design. These two movements, with designers like Gerrit Rietveld, Marcel Breuer, Walter Gropius and Anni Albers, paved the way for a whole new twentieth-century aesthetic, sweeping convention aside.

With the stuffy Victorian design convention firmly consigned to history, the international design movement that would become known as Streamline Moderne arrived on the scene, via art deco. art deco is the name applied retrospectively in the 1960s to a design genre that became widely known following the 1925 Paris Exposition. It appeared in architecture, interior design, graphic design and jewellery, and its signature forms were sweeping curves and sleek, parallel horizontals, often accentuated with polished chrome.

The Streamline Moderne style was clearly influenced by art deco but in a simplified, less ornamented form, with muted colours and a sleek, metallic, futuristic appearance. New materials and innovative uses of existing materials, such as Bakelite, Vitrolite, Formica, enamel, Rexine, glass blocks, aluminium, chrome, and stainless steel replaced iron, timber and brick.

The public desire for all things streamlined would affect the design of every mode of transport, as well as extending to mundane, static objects like toasters and fridges. Some companies made a direct comparison in their advertising between truly streamlined high-speed machines and the everyday household products that mimicked them. Western Brass Mills of Illinois, in one of its posters, illustrated the aesthetic similarities between the wartime, death-dealing torpedoes it manufactured and its peacetime toasters. The intimation was that owning such modern, streamlined products would streamline the lifestyle of a household. The glamour-obsessed 1920s and 1930s was a golden era of industrial design and public relations, in which advertisers used streamlined style as a metaphor for a hygienic, frictionless modern society, free from chaos.

Designers in the USA strove to give an American identity to their aesthetic, using cheaper, modern materials and mass production. Streamlined shapes were ideal for such scales of production in new materials such as the early plastics, like Bakelite.

Streamlining brought modernity and glamour to product design. Designers like Raymond Loewy streamlined everything from locomotives to pencil sharpeners. For Loewy, streamlining was a natural progression, a direction in which aesthetics simply had to go. In 1930 he produced a Chart of the Evolution of Design, which showed how, over time and into an exciting new future, the shapes of a car, a railway carriage, a phone, a clock, a chair, and even a swimming costume were becoming increasingly minimal and streamlined.

In America in particular, where the style was known as Streamform, it became something of a gimmick, a superficial disguise on mundane objects. This fad was a practice vehemently opposed by Henry Dreyfuss, for whom the purpose of streamlining was to reduce wind resistance to increase economy and speed and in some quarters it became known as the 'efficiency aesthetic'. In many cases though, streamlining had little effect on the performance of the product to which it was applied, and was often purely an aesthetic addition.

We must make a distinction, therefore, between the Streamline Moderne design movement, which was mostly about the aesthetic, and true streamlining for aerodynamic efficiency. Of course, many vehicles combined both qualities.

This new interwar aesthetic was a visual breath of fresh air blowing through the stifling poverty and bleak misery that was portrayed so graphically in John Steinbeck's *The Grapes of Wrath*. It was against this background that designers on both sides of the Atlantic became obsessed by the unprecedented power and speed that was possible through advances in technology. This exciting new machine age was a time of ever faster, more glamorous cars, ships, aircraft and trains, and as with the celluloid output of Hollywood at the time, the latest products of the new age were a welcome diversion. Sales were boosted by the manufacture and marketing of products that were more stylish and desirable than ever before.

The theme of the 1939 New York World's Fair was 'Building the World of Tomorrow'. In this world, streamline style was everywhere, including the design of the specially built pavilions. General Motors had its own *Highways and Horizons* pavilion, featuring Norman Bel Geddes' *Futurama* exhibit, a scale model of his *City of 1960*. This bold, utopian vision of the future consisted of streamlined GM cars speeding along broad motorways with sweeping, radiused intersections between graceful, elegant skyscrapers. In *From Submarines to Suburbs: Selling a Better America, 1939–1959*, Cynthia Lee Henthorn describes Bel Geddes' streamlined future as the healthy antithesis to squalor.

The New York World's Fair of 1939 showcased all that was best in streamlining. The people in this image are queueing on the *Helicline*, which passes through the base of the landmark *Trylon* and leads into the *Perisphere*, containing Henry Dreyfuss' *City of Tomorrow* and Raymond Loewy's *Transportation of Tomorrow* exhibits. (John Van Noate collection)

The focal point of the World's Fair was the 600-foot *Trylon*, a futuristic landmark drawing attention to the neighbouring 180-foot diameter *Perisphere*, containing Henry Dreyfuss' *City of Tomorrow*. Also inside was Raymond Loewy's *Transportation of Tomorrow* exhibition of yet more streamlined vehicles and even a Transatlantic rocket ship.

Streamlining had begun to reach the masses through innovative automotive design between the wars, but its origins go back more than two hundred years.

In 1804, Sir George Cayley, a British pioneer of aeronautical engineering, described the ideal streamlined form as 'a very oblong spheroid'. Sixty years later, Revd Dr Samuel Calthrop, an Englishman who had settled in Syracuse, New York, patented an 'air-resisting train', which looked incredibly advanced for the mid-Victorian era. Anticipating many of the features of twentieth-century streamliners, its wheels were completely enclosed, with openings in the steel fairings for maintenance. All passenger doors and windows were closed and the compartment would be cooled by air forced through tubes. This is possibly the earliest mention of any form of air conditioning!

The science of aerodynamics was aided greatly by the advent of the wind tunnel, an enclosed chamber through which air is forced by a fan. The drag coefficient (put simply, wind resistance) of a prototype vehicle can be measured in this controlled environment, as the flow of air past the prototype is observed, in much the same way that Charles Parsons tested his turbine blade profiles in flowing water.

Frank H. Wenham of Britain's Aeronautical Society built the first operational wind tunnel in 1871. He measured lift and drag forces on a series of aerofoil shapes, and his results were significant in the development of aeronautical engineering. He proved that the

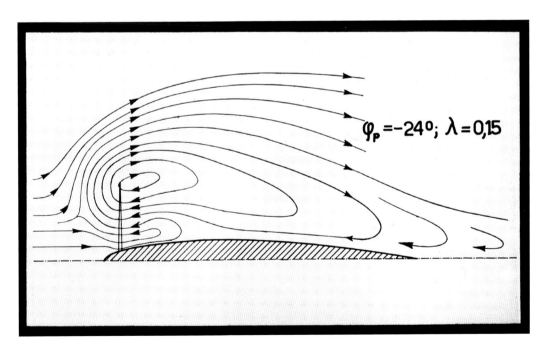

Illustrating the kind of science that would revolutionise streamlining, this diagram shows the pattern of air resistance acting on an aerofoil. Engineers studied how the flow of air in a wind tunnel acted upon an object, and developed their designs through drawings like this. (ETH Zürich)

The body and windows of this Mercedes-Benz, designed by Paul Jaray, Hungarian pioneer of streamlining, have been marked with tape to indicate the direction of airflow in wind-tunnel testing. (ETH Zürich)

lift generated by wings could support substantial loads, a discovery that would lead to the development of powered flight, which had previously seemed almost impossible.

Streamlining was popularised in the 1932 book *Horizons* by American designer Norman Bel Geddes, who applied the principle to automobiles and aircraft. Even slow-moving ships took on some of the elements of streamlined design, mainly to keep up with the style of other forms of transport.

The French called it *Style Paquebot*, or Ocean-liner style, as seen in the design of the luxurious SS *Normandie* of 1932. Indeed, many art deco and streamline products that were firmly rooted on dry land incorporated a nautical influence in their design. One of the most striking features of *Normandie* was the installation of electrically lit glass pillars, designed by René Lalique, in her first-class dining room, a focal point of the art deco interior designed by Pierre Patout. Patout had been a pioneer of art deco architecture and had previously designed the interiors of two other notable liners, the *Ile-de-France* of 1926, and *l'Atlantique* of 1930.

Some of the best-known manifestations of streamlining were on the railways, with beautiful locomotives in daring colour schemes hauling prestigious named expresses. They included the Fliegender Hamburger diesel train in Germany, the American *Hiawatha* and of course Sir Nigel Gresley's A4 Class, on which the streamlined casing and internal streamlining famously helped one of them to break the world speed record for steam, which stands to this day.

The idea of streamlining made even more sense in the air, where the great elongated airships were plying their trade, and aircraft like the Douglas DC-3 cut through the air more easily than anything before. Following the success of the Wright brothers in making

Sir Nigel Gresley's beautiful A4 Class locomotives are synonymous with internal and external streamlining. This helped one of them, *Mallard*, to capture and retain the world speed record for steam, reaching 126 mph. Sister engine No. 60009 *Union of South Africa* has the much more sedate task of heading a Rawtenstall-bound service out of Ramsbottom on the preserved East Lancashire Railway in 2019. (Colin Alexander)

the first successful powered, manned flight, aircraft of the next two decades were mostly biplanes and triplanes of boxkite form. Orville Wright once said, 'If birds can glide for long periods of time, then why can't I?' Several centuries earlier, Leonardo Da Vinci had designed several flying machines after he had studied the flight of birds. The great Italian polymath may have realised that evolution had given the swiftest birds a sleek, streamlined form, but it was not until the 1920s that the same kind of biomimicry practised by Parsons with his trout shapes was applied to aeronautical design. The study of the movement of marine mammals was used to influence the shape of aeroplane fuselages, even though water and air passing by a moving object do not behave in the same way.

By the 1920s it was apparent that streamlining made aircraft fly more efficiently and the science of aerodynamics transformed aircraft design. Perhaps influenced by Germany's Zeppelin airships of the First World War, winged aircraft increasingly featured streamlined fuselages and wing profiles. Aeroplane parts that previously lacked any styling at all, such as engines and undercarriage, suddenly sported streamlined cowlings, as seen on Amelia Earhart's Lockheed Vega, in which she flew solo across the Atlantic Ocean. The streamlining vogue reached an interwar culmination in the sleekly modern Douglas DC-3, which became an icon of the movement. Its profile was synonymous with speed and glamour, influencing the way aircraft looked for decades. Its dynamic look, and that of other streamlined aircraft, captured the imagination of designers and the public alike.

As the skies began to fill with sleek and shiny aircraft that would not look out of place in *Flash Gordon* or Fritz Lang's *Metropolis*, it was not long before Model T Fords and Victorian steam locomotives were sharing the roads and rails of the world with some incredible visions of a streamlined future.

Of course, the Second World War would change everything, permanently. When manufacturing resumed after the war, the streamlined machine age had been replaced by the atomic age, and the styling of vehicles and products continued to evolve. We have not forgotten the legacy of the age of streamlining, or its promise of a better, faster, more beautiful future.

In this book I shall attempt to tell the story of the streamline era, its designers, some of its successes and some of its failures.

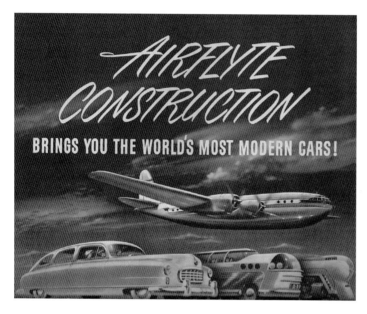

In their advertising, American manufacturers were quick to capitalise on the popularity of streamlining. The Nash Airflyte is seen here alongside a futuristic bus and a Raymond Loewy locomotive, all of which are speeding along below a Boeing Stratocruiser. (John Lloyd collection)

Streamlined automobiles of the 1930s were streamlined throughout, down to the instruments on the dash, the lights and even the lettering of their badges. These tours de force of engineering and aesthetics were a real showcase for multi-talented designers. (John Lloyd)

2

Streamlining on the Road

The earliest internal-combustion-engined road vehicles could not reach any speed at which aerodynamics was a factor. As bigger, more powerful engines were developed, maximum speeds increased and the perpendicular, slab-fronted, flat-windscreen style of the Edwardian era would create excessive wind resistance.

It was understood, if not entirely scientifically, long before the first motor cars ran that wind resistance was a hindrance both to speed and economy.

Late Victorian and Edwardian automotive engineers, early racing drivers and entrepreneurs realised the potential that lay in aerodynamic efficiency, and their experiments resulted in some of the most extraordinary cars ever seen. Today we take aerodynamics for granted, but it took a long time for the car industry to reach that point.

Those daredevils whose goal it was to break the land speed record would constantly strive for aerodynamic advantages over their rivals, and it was in this field that streamlining first

Exemplifying the aesthetics of transport in the days before streamlining changed the way things moved, this 1910 Armstrong Whitworth (actually a replica) at the excellent Beamish Museum in County Durham could hardly be less aerodynamic if it tried. (Colin Alexander)

Imagine being Belgian daredevil Camille Jenatzy in 1899, sitting bolt upright in his bullet-shaped *La Jamais Contente* at 100 kmph! She makes an interesting comparison with one of her near contemporaries in the Cité de l'Automobile in Mulhouse, France. (Paul Aroïd)

appeared on the road. Belgian Camille Jenatzy's *La Jamais Contente* of 1899 was an example of a vehicle that was way ahead of its time. Not only did her bullet-shaped profile allow her to become the first car to attain 100 kmph (62 mph), but she could also boast zero carbon emissions, being all-electric. It must have been mildly terrifying for Jenatzy, sitting exposed like an upright canoeist at a mile a minute, not to mention the effect his torso would have had on the car's aerodynamics! The little car's name translates as **'the never satisfied'**, which aptly describes our obsessive need to reach ever-higher speeds.

As one would expect, the pursuit of the land speed record led to rapid improvements in aerodynamic efficiency in the design of cars whose sole purpose was an entry in the record

From the electric *La Jamais Contente* to the steam-propelled Stanley Rocket of 1906, it would be some years before the internal combustion engine caught up, speedwise. Much lower slung than the Belgian bullet, it topped 200 kmph. (ETH Zürich)

books. The Stanley Steamer Rocket of 1906 was longer and lower than Jenatzy's electric bullet, and only the top of the driver's head was above the profile of the vehicle. She was steam-propelled and was the first to break the 200 kmph barrier, with a maximum of 205 kmph (127 mph), a speed that would not be bettered until 1922.

John Godfrey Parry-Thomas was a Welshman who went from working for Leyland as an engineer to buying his own record breaker. This was the Higham Special with a massive 27-litre aero engine. He named her *Babs* and after many modifications, took her to his Welsh homeland, to Pendine Sands. On his second attempt, in April 1926, he broke the 170 mph barrier. *Babs* featured a long streamlined bonnet and an elongated, tapered tail.

Babs' massive engine and streamlined body took Welshman John Godfrey Parry-Thomas to 170 mph on Pendine Sands in 1926. The car may be admired today in the fascinating Brooklands Museum. (Colin Alexander)

Henry Segrave's incredible, dramatically streamlined record-breaking *Golden Arrow* at the National Motor Museum, Beaulieu. (Karen Roe)

A far more striking foray into streamlining was the Irving-Napier *Golden Arrow*, driven by Henry Segrave to a new world record of 231 mph at Daytona Beach, Florida, in 1929. The car had a very low centre of gravity, achieved by its use of twin propeller shafts on either side of the central driving position. It was a very futuristic-looking vehicle with its pronounced fins and ribs and tapers, all in a sparkling metallic gold finish.

The name most associated with speed records though is that of Campbell, father and son Malcolm and Donald, and their various incarnations of vehicles named *Bluebird*. Malcolm Campbell's Rolls-Royce-powered *Bluebird V* broke the 300 mph barrier in 1935. While the car's staggering 2300 hp output had a lot to do with that feat, she was helped by her advanced streamlined shape with tapered tail and prominent fin.

Aside from the record-breakers, among the first streamlined passenger cars was a one-off Alfa Romeo of 1913 with an incredible teardrop-shaped body, designed by long-established Milan coachbuilder Carrozzeria Castagna for Count Ricotti. Looking like something from the imagination of Jules Verne, it was a prime example of streamlining for visual effect, as the weight of the bodywork negated any aerodynamic benefit. The curved glass, the circular windows and horizontal mudguards were all portents of the future, along with the tiny, beautifully streamlined sidelights that echo the shape of the car. These contrast

Malcolm Campbell's *Bluebird V,* with her smooth contours and tailfin, broke the 300 mph barrier in 1935. This impressive full-size replica is part of the Campbell Bluebird exhibition at the Lakeland Motor Museum in Cumbria. (Colin Alexander)

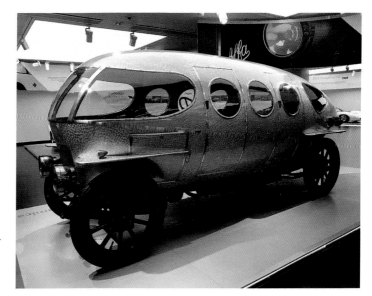

In contrast to the record breakers we have seen, the beautiful Alfa Castagna of 1913 was built as a passenger vehicle, and is a strange mix of past and future. (Angelo Colantonio)

sharply with the outsized, anachronistic main headlamps and rear-mounted horns, along with the antiquated spoked wheels. Count Ricotti would certainly have turned a few heads on the roads of Lombardy.

The real breakthrough in automotive aerodynamics came in 1921 with the appearance of the highly influential German Rumpler Tropfenwagen ('teardrop car'). Whereas Castagna's Alfa was a heavy body-shell grafted onto an existing chassis, the Rumpler was engineered holistically, from scratch. In an early example of cross-disciplinary design, Austrian-born aeronautical engineer Edmund Rumpler patented the advanced independent suspension that carried its airy, mid-engined body with aeroplane-like wings over the wheels. The car featured in Fritz Lang's *Metropolis*, his 1927 cinematic vision of the future. In 1979, when a Tropfenwagen was tested in Volkswagen's Wolfsburg wind tunnel, the drag

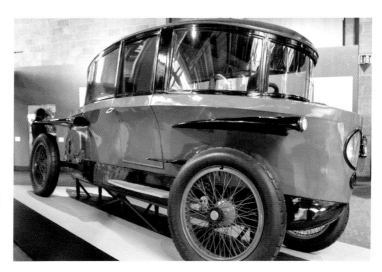

This was the first road car to take streamlining seriously. Edmund Rumpler's Tropfenwagen of 1921 is now displayed in the Deutsches Technikmuseum in Berlin. (Michael Zacher)

coefficient of Rumpler's masterpiece was measured at a slippery 0.28. To put this in context, Volkswagen's own Passat did not match that figure until 1988, and a typical bullet is slightly more resistant to the air at around 0.295!

It would be many years before the innovative Tropfenwagen had any influence on production cars for the masses, but in the world of motor racing its impact was immediate and enduring. The Benz Tropfenwagen racing car of 1923 was a direct descendant, incorporating Rumpler components. It too was built around a mid-positioned engine with swing-axles at the rear, and was the direct ancestor of all subsequent mid-engined racing cars, including the legendary Auto-Unions of the 1930s, engineered by Ferdinand Porsche, about whom there will be more later.

It was another aeronautical engineer who would finally bring streamlining into the world of popular motoring by applying aerodynamic principles to modern production cars. He was Hungarian Paul Jaray, who developed his knowledge of aerodynamics while working at Luftschiffbau Zeppelin. He had been responsible for refining the curving, tapered profile of the 1919 airship LZ120 *Bodensee* in the company's wind tunnel. Its shape was a departure from the long, cylindrical Zeppelins of the First World War.

In 1927, Jaray patented a formula for automotive aerodynamic design principles, which would prove influential. Several manufacturers, including Opel, Maybach and Mercedes, paid for the use of streamlined, Jaray-licensed bodies during the early 1930s.

His early designs, like the Rumpler, were disproportionately tall considering their aerodynamic pretences, but his designs gradually became more conventional in proportion.

A typical example of an early Jaray-designed streamliner was this 1927 Chrysler, coach-built by Haizer Herrmann in Zürich. His vehicles were noted for their unusually tall proportions. (ETH Zürich)

Despite Jaray's scientific approach to aerodynamics, his work was somewhat wasted on these cars, as just like the old Castagna Alfa, they were simply existing rear-wheel drive chassis carrying streamlined bodies.

Other designers, meanwhile, were picking up where Rumpler, with his totally integrated approach, had left off. One such was Scotsman Sir Charles Dennistoun Burney, designer of seaplanes, weapons and sonar systems. His 1930 Streamline car was clearly influenced more by Rumpler than by Jaray. Very unusually for the time, it was powered by a rear engine and like the Tropfenwagen, it was carried on independent suspension.

Burney was managing director of the Airship Guarantee Company in Howden, Yorkshire, which developed the R100 Airship. Sir Charles saw the shape of the airship, with its designed top speed of 70 mph, and used the shape and some of its engineering principles as a basis to design a car of reduced weight and drag compared to its contemporaries.

A more refined, lower-slung example of Jaray styling is the Czech Jawa Sportwagen of 1934, with its striking integral tailfin. (ETH Zürich)

Jaray's Jawa clearly had an influence on the shape of the Maybach SW35 *Stromlinien* Limousine, which appeared the following year. (ETH Zürich)

The Burney Streamline prototype turned heads in Howden, Yorkshire, on test. This example, belonging to the Prince of Wales, is doing the same to a wider audience on the streets of London. (Matt Hatton collection)

The Streamline prototype incorporated leftover airship materials, including aluminium and balloon fabric, and was a local sensation when it was test driven.

Burney's target market was the rich and famous in London, and twelve production vehicles were built in Maidenhead. He intended the car to promote his ideas, in order to encourage the British motor industry to use his patents under licence.

A notable owner of a Burney Streamline was the Prince of Wales, who would become King Edward VIII, and the design was later developed by Crossley, who built another twenty-five similar cars. One of these, the sole survivor, is owned by Lord Montagu of Beaulieu and it is kept at the National Motor Museum.

The motor manufacturer most inextricably linked with streamlining was the Czech firm of Tatra. The cars they produced were hugely influential, and the Tatra became a template for streamlined cars all over the world. One of Tatra's principal designers was Austrian Hans Ledwinka. He took over as chief design engineer in 1921, and he developed a series of highly advanced streamliners with platform frames, independent suspension and rear-mounted air-cooled engines.

One of the most important Tatra models was the compact V570 of 1933, the shape of which was clearly influenced by Jaray. The similarities between this machine and a certain little car being developed by Ferdinand Porsche at the same time are remarkable.

This was a time of rapid progress in the development of streamlined cars, and the visual elements of the most innovative cars of the time were imitated by designers on both sides of the Atlantic. One of the most groundbreaking designs was a 1934 prototype American rear-engined saloon by Dutchman John Tjaarda. Not only did Porsche's KdF-Wagen (later

This influential little car was years ahead of its time in so many ways. The Tatra V570 is seen here displayed in the Salon Retro Mobile in Paris. (Christian Agnes)

known as the Volkswagen Beetle) bear a strong resemblance to the aforementioned Tatra V570, it also echoed Tjaarda's 1934 prototype, especially in the shaping of the front. Erwin Komenda, who was responsible for much of the iconic German vehicle's design, admitted being influenced by it, in a rare example of America influencing European practice.

It was at the 1933/4 Chicago Century of Progress World's Fair that streamlining caused a sensation among the American public and press, as several startling new automobiles hit the market, most notably the Chrysler Airflow. It was low and wide, compared to earlier cars, with the curves, slopes and horizontal elements so typical of the new movement. It was the first truly streamlined American car, and its development began in 1930.

Its designers were Chrysler's Owen Skelton, Carl Breer and Fred Zeder, known as 'The Three Musketeers'. They painstakingly carried out aerodynamic testing of a series of wooden models in a small wind tunnel designed with the cooperation of none other than Orville Wright. This was, in fact, the first wind tunnel to be used by any of the Detroit car manufacturers. They discovered that the conventional, upright 'two-box' car was actually aerodynamically more efficient when travelling backwards! This gave some marketing genius at Chrysler an idea for a publicity stunt in connection with the launch of the new car, as a conventional De Soto sedan was driven all over the United States in reverse!

By 1932 the trio had produced a running prototype that showcased their ideas for streamlining. In order to achieve the sloping rear without compromising interior space, the engine was situated over the front axle. The passenger compartment was well forward, resulting in a short, wide bonnet that curved down to the front bumper. Its headlights were flush with the bodywork and the smooth lines continued over the steeply raked, curved windscreen and across the roof before plunging down the sloping tailend. Inside, the Airflow's dashboard instruments were of a complementary art deco design.

The prototype was demonstrated to Walter Chrysler in secrecy at a location in northern Michigan, and he was so impressed he gave the go-ahead for its development and production. It was a *tour de force* of automotive engineering, incorporating many innovations, and not solely in terms of its aerodynamics. Previously, car bodies had their steel panels fixed to a wooden framework. The Airflow was all-steel, reinforced by latticework. An automatic overdrive in the gearbox saved fuel.

It was, sadly, the styling of the car that was its commercial downfall, for it was simply too innovative for the cautious domestic market. In particular the front end, with the radiator grille integrated in the curving bonnet, was too much of a departure for most American car buyers, and later models had a modified, more upright grille. The Airflow's design was more admired by Europeans, and was widely imitated on this side of the Atlantic. The 1935 Peugeot 402, for example, is clearly influenced by the Airflow, with an even more daring radiator containing its headlights, as if inside a cage.

Ask any petrolhead to name an early streamliner and chances are they will mention the Chrysler Airflow. This 1934 model is displayed in the Gilmore Museum, Hickory Corners, Michigan. (John Lloyd)

The influence of Detroit on European stylists is plain to see on the 1935 Peugeot 402 with its caged-in headlights. (Fabien Canela)

Perhaps one of the most beautiful European essays in streamlined cars was the French Talbot-Lago T-150C SS Coupé of 1937, which gained the nickname *Goutte d'Eau* (drop of water or teardrop). She was designed by Giuseppe Figoni, and is the epitome of art deco style translated into engineered, streamlined beauty.

This is a replica of the beautiful Talbot Lago 'Teardrop' Special Coupé, at Castle Combe in 2015. (Chris Williams)

Despite the unpopularity of the pioneering Chrysler Airflow among an American public that was conservative in its tastes, by 1940 almost all new American cars shared many of the Airflow's pioneering features.

The Cord 810 of 1935 was such an important aesthetic milestone that it was selected as a design icon in 1951 for New York's Museum of Modern Art. The Cord is instantly recognisable with its bold parallel horizontal lines, its aerodynamic styling and lack of unnecessary ornamentation. It was designed by Gordon Buehrig, who also designed automobiles for Auburn and Duesenberg. The 810 was not only futuristic on the outside, though, for it was a very early example of front-wheel drive. Buehrig was influenced not only by fellow transportation designers like Bel Geddes and Loewy, but also the architect Le Corbusier.

Another exhibit at the Gilmore Museum, Hickory Corners, Michigan, is the stunning Cord Beverly, with its trademark horizontal fluting wrapped around the front, and pop-up headlights. (John Lloyd)

Slightly more conventional than the Airflow and the Cord, the Lincoln Zephyr was still a huge aerodynamic advancement over cars of a decade earlier. This 1937 two-door coupé is in the Gilmore Museum. (John Lloyd)

John Tjaarda's rear-engined 1934 prototype, meanwhile, had evolved into the more conventional 1936 Lincoln Zephyr, with front engine housed under a fairly standard bonnet and radiator.

Right and below: Two views of the incredible and rare Stout Scarab, a beautifully kept example of which is seen here at the Hampton Court Concours of Elegance in September 2019. Every little design detail is typical of the streamline era. (Bill Williams)

Another case of an aeronautical engineer becoming involved in automotive design, resulting in a much more interesting and advanced vehicle than the Lincoln Zephyr, was that of the rear-engined Stout Scarab. William Bushnell Stout designed what could be considered the world's first MPV, with an unusual streamlined monocoque body with art deco motifs and a downward-curving rear grille not unlike the front of the much-maligned Airflow. The spacious interior featured seats that could be rotated to face inwards, just like today's minivans. The first Scarab appeared in 1932 but it was not a commercial success due to its high retail price. Stout was also a journalist who wrote a feature on none other than Buckminster Fuller, the great American inventor responsible for another remarkable vehicle. Fuller was way ahead of his time in so many ways, striving for design solutions to global problems, such as housing, energy, environmental issues and poverty. He was responsible for twenty-eight patents including his most well-known invention, the geodesic dome.

Fuller's automotive brainchild was an even more unusual streamliner than the Scarab. His teardrop-shaped, aluminium-bodied Dymaxion was steered by its single rear wheel and boasted an enviably tight turning circle. It could carry eleven people and Fuller's intention was eventually to develop it into a flying vehicle, using jet propulsion. He also designed the Dymaxion house, about which there will be more later.

Meanwhile, in former Czechoslovakia, Tatra's designers had moved on from the landmark V570 to larger vehicles such as the 1934 T77, recognised as the world's first quantity-manufactured streamlined car. Incredibly, the T77 was found to have a drag coefficient of 0.212, a figure that would not be bettered in a production car for sixty years, until General Motors' EV-1 of 1995. The T77 began a long line of V8-powered, air-cooled streamliners that were capable of 100 mph on the new autobahns of Third Reich Germany.

Only three examples of Buckminster Fuller's groundbreaking 1933 Dymaxion were built at the time. This replica was built by architect Norman Foster, and it is seen here at Goodwood House in Sussex. (Helen Sanders)

This photograph taken at the Tatra Register Nederland Annual Rally near Roosendaal, Netherlands, allows us to compare two of the streamlined Czech beauties, built thirty-two years apart. The red model 603 dates from 1971 and the silver T87 from 1939. (Peter Visser)

They were very popular with high-ranking officers of the Luftwaffe. Like many early rear-engined cars, however, they had a tendency to oversteer, and the T77 became known as the 'Czech secret weapon', as several key figures in Hitler's regime died at the wheel, leading him supposedly to ban it!

Was there ever a car as smooth and slippery as the Schlörwagen? It seems remarkable that this vehicle appeared before the Second World War. (DLR German Aerospace Center)

In terms of aerodynamics, the T77 was positively box-like compared to the experimental German Schlörwagen of 1939. Engineer Karl Schlör of the Aerodynamischen Versuchsanstalt built it around a 38 hp Mercedes. The body, designed for seven passengers, was based on the profile of aircraft wings and he ensured that all windows were flush with the body. The car appeared at the 1939 Berlin Motor Show, where it was nicknamed the 'Göttingen Egg'. It was 20 mph faster than the original Mercedes and was up to 40 percent more economical on fuel. Its phenomenal drag coefficient of 0.15 is beaten only by modern vehicles such as Volkswagen's hybrid XL1, and certainly not by any seven-seaters!

So the 1930s was a defining decade for automotive design, during which time the car evolved from its horse-drawn ancestry into an integrally engineered, aerodynamic, desirable product to meet the demands of the public. This was true nowhere more than in Germany, where the first autobahns were being opened.

Despite Hitler's ban on the Tatra for his officers, its styling clearly had an effect on him, for he specifically named the Czech vehicle as an example to follow when he asked Ferdinand Porsche to design him a people's car. The streamlined shape of the resulting Volkswagen KdF, the prototype for the legendary 'Beetle', was designed with the autobahn in mind. Ferdinand Porsche thought that an engine delivering 20 hp would propel the car at 100 kmph as long as it was aerodynamic enough, and so it was. The little VW probably had as much of an influence on post-war automotive design as all of the more glamorous streamliners put together.

The Volkswagen would also evolve into one of the most iconic cars of all time, the Porsche 356. Predating the 356 by almost a decade, though, was Ferdinand Porsche's sports-car version of the Beetle, the Type 64.

Porsche's Austrian designers Erwin Komenda, Karl Froelich and Josef Mickl had previously collaborated on the KdF and the legendary Auto Union racing cars. One of

The Volkswagen KdF-Wagen would of course become known as the Beetle or the Bug, becoming the most numerous car on the planet. It continued in production in Mexico until 2003. (Mark Rayf)

The astonishing, curvaceous Auto Union Rekordwagen of 1937. (ETH Zürich)

This replica of the 1939 Porsche Type 64 was on loan to the Petersen Auto Museum in Los Angeles from the Prototype Museum in Hamburg. Only three were built, and this replica incorporates original Type 64 components. (Jon Rapp)

the latter, the Type C streamliner of 1937, was driven by Bernd Rosemeyer to a speed of 236 mph. The Austrian engineers would go on to design a series of grand prix racing cars and several Porsche models including the 356.

The catalyst that led to the building of the Type 64 prototype was a 1,500 km race from Berlin to Rome to be staged in September 1939. A wooden scale prototype, tested in the wind tunnel at Stuttgart University, evolved into a lightweight car with a riveted alloy body which owed much to aeronautical practice.

The outbreak of the Second World War put paid to the 1939 race and it would be the late 1940s before production began on the illustrious descendant of the Type 64, the Porsche 356. This amazing little vehicle was the first production Porsche sports car. The combination of lightweight aluminium body and streamlining derived from experience with the Type 64 meant its 1.1-litre rear-mounted engine could push it over 80 mph.

Mercedes-Benz also built a car for the Berlin to Rome race. This was the one-off aluminium-bodied 540K streamliner of 1938, which was designed as a high-speed test vehicle for Dunlop tyres in Germany. This beautiful silver car was recently restored and is a miraculous survivor.

Another notable European 'people's car' whose development was arrested by war was the little Citroën 2CV. Pierre Boulanger's 'umbrella on four wheels' emerged in 1937 as a crude prototype, but with a streamlined shape to maximise performance from its tiny air-cooled engine. Its closest rival, the Renault 4, was aesthetically a veritable box on wheels. The 1948 production model was more refined and was a great success, bringing motoring to a whole new market. It continued in production until 1990.

There are two other illustrious Citroëns worthy of inclusion here. One is the Traction Avant, a low-slung, raked-back saloon of 1934 with advanced front-wheel drive and an aerodynamic body. Groundbreaking as this car was in so many ways, it was nothing compared to its 1955 successor, the technological masterpiece that was the DS, whose drag coefficient equals that of the Ferrari Testarossa, thirty years its junior.

Also displayed in LA's Petersen Auto Museum is the beautiful 1958 Porsche 356A 1600 Super Speedster 1a. (Jon Rapp)

Intended for the 1938 Berlin to Paris race, the recently restored, unique Mercedes-Benz 540K Streamliner is a remarkable and precious survivor. (Edward Stump)

In stark contrast to its German contemporary above, Pierre Boulanger's utilitarian 1937 prototype Citroën 2CV is seen here in the Design Museum in London. She may look crude but her streamlined body helped her extract the maximum performance and economy from her tiny air-cooled engine. (Colin Alexander)

Above: The low, rakish Citroën Traction Avant, launched in 1934. (Colin Alexander)

Below: The 1950s Citroën DS was as aerodynamic as a 1980s Ferrari. (Colin Alexander)

A lesser-known car than the DS, but every bit as futuristic, was the Phantom Corsair, which predated the French beauty by seventeen years. Rust Heinz was the grandson of Henry J. Heinz, founder of the canned food giant. Rust moved on from studying yacht design and set up a studio, trying to establish himself as an automotive designer. He produced a prototype for a bespoke delivery vehicle for the family firm, a revolutionary teardrop-shaped van called the Comet, complete with the famous '57' logo on the side.

From this he moved on to what he hoped would be the first American supercar. An incredibly sleek, aerodynamic clay model was taken to Christian Bohman and Maurice Schwartz, Californian coachbuilders of Swedish and Austrian birth respectively. They built Heinz's vision of the future on a custom-built front-wheel-drive chassis powered by a Cord V8 engine, which took the slippery shark-of-the-road up to 115 mph.

The Phantom Corsair was designed to carry six passengers, four in the front and two behind. It featured aviation-style instrumentation, push-button automatic doors, tinted safety glass, and hydraulic bumpers. This car wasn't years ahead of its time, it was decades ahead.

Heinz's streamlined masterpiece was named 'The Car of Tomorrow' at the World's Fair, and featured in a full-page advertisement in Esquire magazine. It was an early example of product placement when the car played *The Flying Wombat* in David O. Selznick's 1938 comedy film *The Young in Heart*, and it also appeared in the Popular Science film series. In spite of all of this, no orders were forthcoming and the Phantom Corsair was destined to remain an expensive one-off.

Thankfully, Rust Heinz's stunning and unique 1938 Phantom Corsair survives in the Bill Harrah collection. It can usually be admired in the National Automobile Museum in Reno, Nevada, but is seen here at Goodwood Festival of Speed in England, in 2013. (Geoff Buckland)

Perhaps the most outlandish foray into streamline styling on the road happened after the Second World War, at General Motors, under the direction of stylist Harley Earl. The first of many concept cars he created was the visually advanced Buick Y Job of 1938. After the war he was inspired by the aesthetics of the latest jet fighter aircraft, whose dramatic appearance he translated into the design of a series of striking concepts, Firebird I–IV. They were jet-powered and featured the latest aviation control technology. Many of Earl's designs were adorned with exaggerated tail fins and pronounced bumper overriders resembling missiles, and carried an excess of chrome.

One of the more interesting Harley Earl designs was the astonishing Futurliner. Twelve of these remarkable streamlined art deco vehicles were built in 1939 and 1940. They were custom-made for General Motors' travelling exhibition, the Parade of Progress, which set

Just look at all that chrome! Harley Earl's beautiful Buick Y Job, also dating from 1938. (John Lloyd)

Another incredible vision from the drawing board of Harley Earl, this is the General Motors Futurliner mobile exhibition vehicle of 1939. (John Lloyd)

out to promote future technology, and of course GM cars. The Futurliner was an ingenious mobile display stand whose exterior panels opened out to show everything from turbojet engines to microwave ovens, stereos and televisions. Some of Earl's ideas were expressed in America's most iconic cars of the 1950s such as the outrageous rear-end treatment of the Cadillac Eldorado Seville with its enormous fins and rocket ship styling.

None of these styling motifs contributed anything significant to the aerodynamic performance of the vehicle, and his cars were as excessive as Porsche's little 356 was beautifully simple. This contrast is a stark demonstration of the differing directions in which the American and European motor industries were moving, having started their evolutionary journeys through streamlining at the same point.

Milwaukee-based designer Clifford Brooks Stevens, who along with Raymond Loewy and eight others formed the Industrial Designers Society of America, designed a very handsome streamlined motor home, the 1941 Western Flyer.

Right: Harley Earl's ideas led to some of the most iconic American cars such as this 1959 Cadillac Eldorado Seville. (John Lloyd)

Below: Clifford Brooks Stevens was one of the founders of the Industrial Designers Society of America. Among his many streamlined designs was the 1941 Western Flyer motor home. (Greg Gjerdingen)

The fad for streamlining on the roads was not limited to private motoring. The interwar years saw a growth in long-distance bus travel, especially in the United States, where the Greyhound bus was by far the biggest brand, and from 1937, when Raymond Loewy's Supercoach entered service, it became synonymous with modern, streamline-styled vehicles. At that time, the company served 4,750 bus stations, which themselves were given the latest Streamline Moderne treatment. Later vehicles, such as the iconic split-level Scenic Cruiser, were based on Loewy's designs, and these were distinctively clad in reflective, horizontally fluted aluminium.

Above and below: The pioneering Greyhound Super Coach, by Raymond Loewy, and the later iconic split-level Scenic Cruiser. (flickr.com autohistorian)

Across the Atlantic, meanwhile, just as the shape of the Volkswagen had been designed to take advantage of the new autobahns then spreading across Germany, several designs of streamline-bodied buses were entering service.

A particularly attractive example was the 1938 Fritzsche Flöha, a one-off based on the chassis of a burned-out Opel Blitz truck, recovered from a quarry. At the time, the German Reich was gearing up for war so steel was rationed. Despite this, taxi boss Guido Fritzsche expanded his fleet with a remarkable minibus of ultra-modern streamlined shape and fitted with curved windows

A much later experiment, dating from the mid-1950s but worthy of inclusion, was an ambitious bus prototype known as the Golden Dolphin. Designed by Viberti of Turin, it featured a futuristic panoramic plastic body and was to be powered by a gas turbine to reach its intended cruising speed of 125 mph.

Even two-wheeled vehicles were affected by the streamlining craze. The classic Piaggio Vespa scooter of 1945 drew upon the aviation experience of designer Corradino d'Ascanio, who pioneered the use of stressed-skin monocoque construction in its streamlined fairings.

Among the exhibits at the Victoria & Albert Museum's 1946 'Britain Can Make It' event was Ben Bowden's Bicycle of the Future. An employee of the Rootes group of motor manufacturers, he used lightweight alloy for the frames whose streamlined shape was said to be inspired by design elements from the liner RMS *Queen Mary*.

One final category to squeeze in as we make the transition from road to rail, and one on which streamlining was very much a cosmetic exercise for publicity purposes, was the streamlined tram or streetcar. These of course ran on rails that were set into roads. Well-known examples are Blackpool's 'Balloon' double-decker trams, and American PCC streetcars, both dating from the 1930s and both featuring classic elements of streamline style.

An example of an Autobahn Stromlinienbus, this one-off 1938 Opel Blitz is preserved in a Berlin municipal transport depot. (Lars Simon)

This is Viberti's astonishing 125 mph Golden Dolphin bus of the 1950s. (Alon Siton collection)

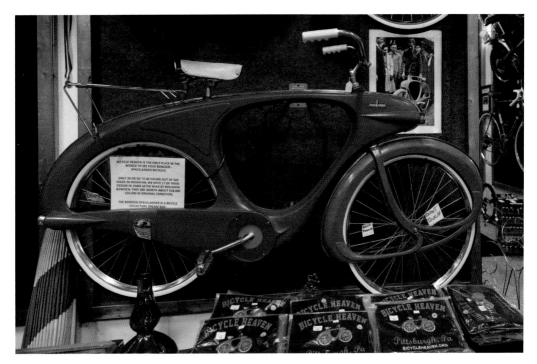

A lovely example of Ben Bowden's Bicycle of the Future in Bicycle Heaven, Pittsburgh, Pennsylvania. (Edward H. Blake)

As the motorists of today speed along the world's interstates, autobahns and motorways in their sleek hybrids and electric cars, we should all spare a thought for those pioneers and engineers from Camille Jenatzy to Ferdinand Porsche, who had such an influence on the aesthetics and aerodynamics of our beloved machines.

Above: This streamlined Blackpool 'Balloon' tram is preserved at Beamish Museum in County Durham. (Colin Alexander)

Below: The classic American streamlined PCC streetcar, as seen in San Francisco. (Colin Alexander)

3

Streamlining on the Rails

Just as convention put a big bonnet at the front of the motor car, steam locomotives had a cylindrical boiler, of increasing diameter and length, ahead of the footplate throughout steam railway history. This arrangement did not lend itself easily to streamlining. By the time the benefits of streamlining, in terms of both performance and public relations, were known, the steam locomotive was already as physically large as it could be, with little room within the loading gauge (the maximum permitted size to pass through bridges, etc.) for streamlined casings.

It was much more practical to streamline diesel and electric trains, where there was more scope to sculpt the exterior without affecting the power unit inside.

Beautiful though she is, Patrick Stirling's Great Northern Railway No. 1 of 1870 is in no way streamlined, with multiple vertical, forward-facing surfaces. Her upright attitude typifies the Victorian steam locomotive. Nevertheless capable of reaching speeds of over 80 mph, she is seen here at her Doncaster birthplace in 2003 alongside a true streamliner. (Colin Alexander)

While the streamlining of cars can reduce drag at high speeds by up to half, the same treatment applied to trains does not have the same effect. Why should the same principle not apply? It is simply that cars are short and trains are long. Most of the air resistance acting on the body shell of a speeding car results from the difference in air pressure on the front profile of the car and that at the back. This is known as 'form drag', and happens as the air moving along the car clings to the vehicle before 'breaking away', leaving lower pressure behind. Whereas the body of a car can taper towards the rear, forcing the boundary layer to cling to the vehicle for as long as possible before breaking away, this is more difficult to achieve with a train. High-speed passenger trains are composed of multiple vehicles and if they tapered along the length of the train towards the rear they would have to be in a fixed formation. Many of the great streamlined trains did feature an aerodynamically profiled rear end but this was mostly for publicity and effect.

In any case, much of the air resistance acting upon a moving train results from air passing beneath the vehicles, and along the sides and roofs, which represents a much larger surface area than the cross-section of the front. This did not stop railway engineers jumping on the aerodynamic bandwagon, and in some notable cases the resulting streamlining did have some effect in improving performance and economy.

One of the earliest essays in railborne streamlining, thirty years after Revd Dr Calthrop's proposed 'air-resisting train', was Charles Baudry's C Class with their distinctive *coupe-vent*, or 'wind-cutting' fairings to smooth out the forward-facing surfaces of the cab, chimney and smokebox. They were built in Paris in 1893 for the Chemins de fer de Paris à Lyon et à la Méditerranée.

Chemins de fer de Paris à Lyon et à la Méditerranée 4-4-0 Co. C23, built by Ateliers de Paris in 1893. She carries extensive *coupe-vent*, or 'wind-cutting' fairings. (Alon Siton collection)

Carrying similar wind-cutting fairings to those fitted to the French 4-4-0, this is the Königlich Bayerischen Staats-Eisenbahnen's experimental 4-4-4 Co. 3201, seen at Nuremberg in 1925. (Alon Siton collection)

Similarly attired, aerodynamically, was the experimental Königlich Bayerischen Staats-Eisenbahnen (Royal Bavarian State Railways) Class S 2/6 No. 3201. Built in 1906, she possessed some highly advanced external features, such as the curved skirt in front of the cylinders, the conical smokebox door, fairings on the chimney and dome, and the wedge-shaped cab front. These additions, together with her superheating and four cylinders, propelled her to a speed of 95.6 mph, not bettered in Germany for thirty years. Despite their use in both France and Bavaria, these streamlined features would not be commonplace until much later in the twentieth century.

This is wind-cutter treatment, American style. Preserved McKeen petrol railcar No. 22 is seen inside the Nevada Railroad Museum, Carson City. The first of these distinctive vehicles appeared in 1905. (Larry Meinstein)

A slightly earlier 'wind-cutter' than the Bavarian locomotive was the McKeen petrol-engined railcar in the United States. The first was built in Nebraska in 1905 and as well as the streamlined profile it anticipated other later streamlining motifs, such as the porthole windows, which were adopted for structural strength.

Other streamlined diesel railcars would follow, including the well-known examples on the Great Western Railway in Britain. They were the invention of C. F. Cleaver of Hardy Railmotors, a subsidiary of the Associated Equipment Co. Ltd (AEC). Cleaver calculated that the trusty AEC diesel engine that was used in London buses would be powerful enough to propel a lightweight single railcar, particularly if it was aerodynamically styled to reduce wind resistance.

Wind tunnel testing was carried out at the London Passenger Transport Board's laboratories, and the resulting shape was an eye-catching, streamlined vehicle.

Railcar No. 1 was bought by the GWR, having been a popular attraction at the 1933 International Commercial Motor Transport Exhibition in London. Its success led to further orders of railcars with twin engines, permitting a maximum speed of 80 mph.

Probably the most famous of the early streamlined diesel units was Germany's Fliegender Hamburger of 1933. This was a two-car set for the prestigious high-speed run from Berlin to Hamburg, which it covered at an average of 77 mph, then the fastest in the world. Again, wind tunnel experimentation had been used to determine the optimum profile of the lightweight, articulated sets, and one of them would reach 133 mph on a test run.

This was not Germany's first essay in streamlined railcars, though. In 1929 aeronautical engineer Franz Kruckenberg's experimental Schienenzeppelin took to the rails. Shaped

The most famous early streamlined railcars in Britain were the AEC-engined diesels on the Great Western Railway. Preserved No. 4 is seen here at Banbury in the 1960s. She now resides inside the National Railway Museum in York with other notable streamliners. (Singen Dommett)

Der Fliegender Hamburger revolutionised rail travel in Germany from 1933, as it had to, to fend off growing competition from commercial aircraft and the new autobahns. This example is preserved in the Deutsche Bahn Museum in Nuremberg. (Ian Black)

like an aeroplane's fuselage and equipped with a rear-mounted propellor, it held the world speed record on the rails for twenty-three years, reaching 143 mph. A more conventional Kruckenberg design was his experimental, lightweight high-speed railcar, built in 1938. Shelved during the war, its outward design clearly influenced the appearance of the 1950s Class VT 11.5 Deutsche Bundesbahn Trans Europ Express multiple units.

Another propellor-driven rail vehicle was George Bennie's extraordinary and futuristic Railplane, which, like the Schienenzeppelin, also debuted in 1929. Bennie built a demonstration overhead monorail at Milngavie, north of Glasgow, on which his Railplane was tried out at speeds of up to a claimed 120 mph. At one time he proposed a similar 200 mph monorail across the Sahara Desert!

Meanwhile, the London & North Eastern Railway was considering a high-speed diesel service on the Newcastle to London route, similar to the Fliegender Hamburger, and the German manufacturers were asked to submit proposals. The best average speed they could offer for their design was 63 mph, slower than its German performance due to speed restrictions and gradients en route. Sir Nigel Gresley, the company's Chief Mechanical Engineer, believed that steam power was superior. To prove it, he arranged a test run in 1934 with his Class A1 No. 4472 *Flying Scotsman*, hauling six coaches, three times the capacity and weight of the German train, from Leeds to the capital. On this run, No. 4472 achieved the world's first authenticated 100 mph by a steam locomotive. A few months later, sister engine No. 2750 *Papyrus*, with higher boiler pressure and classified A3, did

The design of Kruckenberg's experimental high-speed railcar of 1938 led to the shape of the classic 1950s Deutsche Bundesbahn Trans Europ Express trains. (Alon Siton collection)

A vintage postcard depicting the Bennie railplane on its monorail at Milngavie, Scotland. (Colin Alexander collection)

even better on a test run from the capital to Newcastle and back, reaching 108 mph. Gresley knew that a streamlined version could do better still.

This was to be no mere cosmetic exercise, for his A4 Class would be streamlined on the inside, too. The LNER publicised a new four-hour service from Newcastle to London, with an average speed of 67 mph. Always with an eye for publicity, the new train was to be known as the Silver Jubilee, commemorating twenty-five years of the reign of George V, and it carried an eye-catching livery of silver grey. Gresley had studied the French Bugatti Autorail Rapide railcar and used its front profile as the basis of his A4, following wind tunnel testing.

The comparative horsepower needed to overcome the air resistance on a Gresley A1/A3 and that on a streamlined A4 was calculated, and it showed that at a speed of 60 mph, the non-streamlined locomotive needed 97 hp to cut through the air, whereas the A4 needed only 56. At 90 mph the difference was far more pronounced, the A1/A3 requiring a substantial 328 hp, compared to the A4's economical 190 hp.

The A4 was also a great example of the internal streamlining mentioned earlier, for the diameters and curvature and angles of all of the internal pipework, even the smoothness of the surfaces of castings, were designed to permit the smoothest possible flow of high-pressure steam to the cylinders. The shape of the valances over the wheels is the shape of a true aerofoil, as specified by Gresley after he studied drawings of the R101 airship, and an additional benefit of the aerodynamic front end is that at speed, drifting smoke

The streamlined profile of the Bugatti Autorail Rapide railcar of 1934 was studied by Sir Nigel Gresley. This beautiful example is preserved in the Cité du Train, Mulhouse, France. (Andrew Thirlby)

from the chimney was lifted clear of the locomotive crew's vision. The Silver Jubilee was a triumph both mechanically and commercially, leading to the introduction of two further A4-hauled streamlined services, the Coronation and the West Riding Limited. Streamlined 'beavertail' observation cars were provided and fairings were placed between the coaches to reduce wind resistance around corridor connections. On a trial publicity run in 1935 the Silver Jubilee, hauled by first of the class, No. 2509 *Silver Link*, reached the unprecedented speed of 112½ mph.

Above and below: Epitomising the beauty, the glamour and the publicity value of streamlining, Gresley A4 No. 4492 *Dominion of New Zealand*, looks resplendent in her novel garter blue livery with stainless steel Gill Sans lettering. She heads the Coronation train, with its matching beavertail observation car at the rear. (Alon Siton collection)

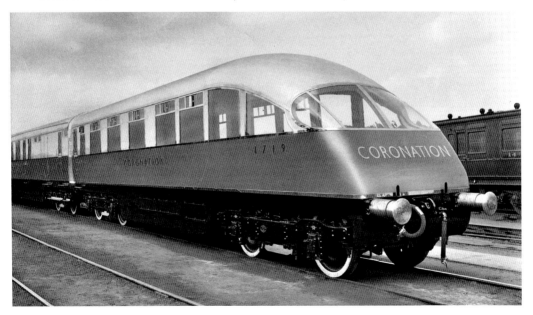

Not to be outdone in the publicity stakes, the LNER's rival for Anglo-Scottish traffic, the London, Midland & Scottish Railway, introduced its own glamorous streamliner in 1937, to be named the *Coronation Scot*. Its Chief Mechanical Engineer was Sir William Stanier, who designed the powerful 'Coronation' Class with four cylinders to cope with the route's more arduous gradients. He was against the idea of streamlining, feeling it was superfluous, but the company wanted a slice of the publicity being enjoyed by the LNER. On a press run, first of the class No. 6220 *Coronation* reached a maximum speed of 114 mph. Sister engine No. 6229 visited the USA and was exhibited as the epitome of British engineering at the aforementioned New York World's Fair of 1939. The bulbous, almost brutal streamlining of the Stanier engines lacked the grace of the A4s, and it was removed by the 1940s, resulting in a very handsome, impressive class of locomotives.

The world speed record had gone to Germany in 1936, when one of three experimental Class 05 streamlined locomotives of the Deutsche Reichsbahn, built by Borsig, attained a

Just as striking as the LNER's streamliners were Stanier's Coronations on the LMSR. This is an official workshop portrait of No. 6241 *City of Edinburgh*. (Alon Siton collection)

Displayed in the Nuremberg Transport Museum is streamliner No. 05.001. Sister engine No. 05.002 held the world steam speed record for a time, before *Mallard* took the crown forever. (Dr Werner Söffing)

speed of 125 mph with a lightweight test train. In appearance, the first two were not unlike Stanier's streamliners, but the third had its cab at the front, using pulverised coal for its fuel. It was later rebuilt along more conventional lines.

Then just before the outbreak of the Second World War, another class of streamliners appeared on the Deutsche Reichsbahn. These were the powerful Class 01.10, totalling fifty-five in number. They were imposing machines but all lost their streamlined casings after the war.

Meanwhile in 1938, back on the LNER, Gresley A4 No 4168 *Mallard* famously broke the world speed record, attaining 126 mph, a maximum that would never be beaten with steam traction.

Incidentally, in 1939, another lesser-known streamliner appeared on the LMSR, in the shape of a three-car articulated diesel railcar with more than a passing resemblance to Der Fliegender Hamburger.

The public relations sensation created by the sleek new Anglo-Scottish expresses left some within the ranks of the Great Western and the Southern Railway feeling that they ought to get in on the streamlining act. As a result, one member of each of the GWR's 'King' and 'Castle' classes was festooned with a hemispherical cover to its smokebox door, and various fairings on the boiler mountings and cab front. The GWR's Chief Mechanical Engineer, Charles Collett, who was responsible for both of these fine classes of locomotive,

This official works photograph shows the experimental German cab-forward No. 05.003, shortly before completion at the Borsig works. She awaits the fitting of glazing to her windows and is as yet unpainted. (Alon Siton collection)

The imposing sight of locomotive No. 01.1001 of the Deutsche Reichsbahn immediately after completion at BMAG/ Schwartzkopff. Note the sovereign eagle on the front. (Alon Siton collection)

wanted nothing to do with the vanity project. He surely knew that any advantage in reducing drag would be offset by the additional weight, and the additions certainly did nothing to improve the appearance of these handsome machines. The streamlining was removed from both engines after a short period in service.

Even more bizarre was the application of streamlining to another successful locomotive type, one of the Southern Railway's excellent 'Schools' Class, designed by Richard Maunsell. No. 935 *Sevenoaks* was the engine selected by Maunsell's successor, Oliver Bulleid, who had worked under Sir Nigel Gresley at Doncaster. He encased her in a smooth plywood shroud, in which she made a round trip from Eastleigh works to Micheldever and back, during which the temporary casing vibrated alarmingly! The plywood was hastily removed. This was not the last of Mr Bulleid's essays in streamlining, or 'air-smoothing' as he preferred to call it.

During the Second World War, locomotive construction was focused on utilitarian workhorses for the war effort, machines that were easy to maintain such as the Stanier 8F. So it was definitely not a time to be building glamorous streamlined express passenger engines. Oliver Bulleid, however, described his new 'Merchant Navy' Class locomotives as

Bulleid's unconventional 'air-smoothing' as seen on preserved West Country Class No. 34092 *City of Wells*, in action at Grosmont, North Yorkshire Moors Railway. (Colin Alexander)

air-smoothed mixed-traffic engines, and somehow got away with it! They were followed by the lighter 'West Country' and 'Battle of Britain' Classes and they were quite unlike any previous British essays in streamlining. The cladding on their sides was almost flat, and the front profile, though raked back, presented a large surface area surmounted by an overhang. This was designed to create a draught that would lift exhaust smoke clear of the locomotive. Most were rebuilt in a more conventional form, losing their air-smoothing. As in the case of Stanier's defrocked streamliners, the result was a very aesthetically pleasing locomotive.

While the Germans had their record-breaking Class 05s, the French had a more numerous series of impressive streamliners of the same 4-6-4 wheel arrangement. They were more graceful in appearance than their rather brutal-looking Teutonic counterparts. One of them can be admired in the railway museum in Mulhouse, the unique No. 232U.1, which was a 1949 rebuild of a partially completed Lungstrom turbine locomotive, whose construction had been interrupted by the war, and based on the prewar S Class. Nicknamed 'The Divine', she was designed by Marc De Caso, and was reputedly one of the best and certainly one of the most handsome French express steam passenger locomotives ever produced.

The magnificent SNCF No. 232.U.1 preserved in the Cité du Train, Mulhouse, France. (Michael Goll)

Elsewhere in Europe, the railway networks of both Czechoslovakia and Poland boasted streamliners too. Czechoslovakia was of course known for its Tatra streamliners on the roads. Another Czech motor car manufacturer is Škoda, which also built locomotives for railways around the world. One of its 1927-built engines, No. 386.001, received streamlining in 1937 similar to that applied to the German Class 05s. She was allocated to Bratislava to haul luxurious express services.

Poland's most numerous class of streamliners originated in Germany as Reichsbahn Class 03s, which were the subject of experiments in streamlining from 1935. They were smooth-running, modern and fast machines of sound design, but during the war, some fell into Soviet hands. Of these, nine were handed over to the Polish authorities, who reclassified the engines as PM3. Despite the poor condition of post-war Polish permanent way, 80 mph was a regular occurrence with these German-built trophies of war.

Peacetime Germany, meanwhile, would go on to become a world leader in the building of lightweight streamlined diesel railcars for its domestic market and for export, continuing the legacy of the Fliegender Hamburger.

Another heroic PR-led attempt at streamlining on a British railway is worthy of mention, this time a 1936 'tube' train cutting through the stale air beneath London, on the Underground's Piccadilly Line. Resembling the Fliegender Hamburger but with a broad flared skirt at platform level, it was a striking design. It featured in the *Middlesex County*

Skoda's one-off Czech streamliner No. 386.001, whose livery closely resembles that applied to Stanier's Coronations. (Alon Siton collection)

One of several former Reichsbahn Class 03 streamliners that was captured by the Soviets and used in Poland. Note the similarity in appearance between this and the Class 01.10 seen earlier. (ETH Zürich)

Times: 'In every way the comfort of the passenger has been studied in this new design ... By placing the [electrical] equipment beneath the floor ... all the space within the train ... can now be used for seating passengers ... Special gears and wheels with new silencing devices have been employed. Pillars between the windows are smaller than usual ... thus enlarging the passenger's outlook.' Of course, with speeds on the Underground never exceeding 60 mph, the exercise was one of pure aesthetics and publicity, and was sadly not perpetuated.

The first purpose-built steam streamliner in the United States was of the unusual (for a streamlined locomotive) wheel arrangement of 4-4-2. They were known as Class A, and were introduced in 1935 specifically for hauling the high-speed Hiawatha service on the Chicago, Milwaukee, St Paul & Pacific Railroad. They were reputedly capable of 120 mph and would regularly reach 100.

Clifford Brooks Stevens, whose streamlined motor home we saw earlier, designed the beautiful Skytop Lounge cars, which from 1948 formed the distinctive tail-end of the Hiawatha. With their multiple windows like the compound eye of an insect, orange livery and chrome band carrying the Hiawatha name in a stylish italic typeface, they rank among the most attractive passenger coaches ever to run on rails.

Another Chicago-based railroad operated what was probably the most famous streamlined train in the USA. This was the Burlington Zephyr of 1934, on the Chicago, Burlington & Quincy Railroad. The sleek new diesel trains featured lightweight, spot-welded stainless steel bodies with horizontal accents along the sides, and aerodynamic fairings over the bogie frames. At the front end, the traditional cowcatcher became an elegant, curved skirt whose profile continued up to the windscreen and roofline. Echoing aeronautical practice,

Another great rail-borne streamlined icon was the Chicago, Milwaukee, St Paul & Pacific Railroad's Hiawatha service. Unusually for streamliners, the locomotives were of a 4-4-2 wheel arrangement. (Alon Siton collection)

Just as the LNER's prestigious new trains were streamlined at both ends, so was the Hiawatha. Clifford Brooks Stevens, whose Western Flyer motor home we saw in the last chapter, designed the distinctive Skytop Lounge car. This beauty is preserved in the Daytona Beach Museum of Arts & Sciences, Florida. (Justin Nelson)

Mail bags are exchanged at Table Rock, Nebraska, as the Burlington Zephyr pauses on the Kansas City to Lincoln, Nebraska route. (Don Melsha)

its advanced monocoque shell was wind tunnel tested, and it was described by designer William Bushnell Stout, of Stout Scarab fame, as the 'wingless aircraft on tracks'. On a record-breaking run from Chicago to Denver, one of the Zephyrs attained 112.5 mph.

Raymond Loewy applied the existing conventions of streamlining to some of the most iconic American locomotives, and added ideas of his own. These included 'speed whiskers', a decorative motif which would be used on railways all over the world until the 1960s.

Among Loewy's most astonishing locomotive designs, indeed one of the most astonishing locomotives ever built, was the Pennsylvania Railroad's one-off 'duplex' classified S.1, with the remarkable wheel arrangement of 6-4-4-6. Her exterior streamlining was pure Loewy. Given the running number 6100, she spent her first couple of years in steam, mounted on rollers at that great exposition of all things futuristic and streamlined, the 1939 New York World's Fair.

The longest non-articulated locomotive ever built, she was designed to haul trains of 1,200 tons at 100 mph, but was too long for most turntables and curves. She was, however, a massive public relations success, not least at the World's Fair, and led to the development of the later T-1s of shorter 4-4-4-4 arrangement. Leading US locomotive builder Baldwin received the order for two of these from the Pennsylvania RR in 1942. In appearance they were truly breathtaking, Raymond Loewy giving them a look that was totally unlike anything seen on the rails before, with a sinister profile not dissimilar to a submarine. They were designed to pull the most prestigious trains, such as the Broadway Limited, and could manage a sixteen-car passenger train at 100 mph.

Loewy's greatest contribution to rail transport was his Pennsylvania Railroad GG1 electric locomotive. Two preserved examples are seen here in 2014 at Boonton Transportation Heritage Festival in New Jersey. (Andy Sutcliffe)

Loewy's most enduring design on America's railroads predated his steam duplexes. It was also on the Pennsylvania RR, and powered not by steam, but by electricity. This was his iconic GG1, of which 139 were built from 1934, and they lasted in service for almost fifty years. The Pennsylvania wanted them to have a unique, streamlined appearance and turned to Loewy. The body was a symphony of curves, with welded panels. The prominent nose ends were adorned with an integral headlight, the PRR totem and sweeping speed whiskers, which would become part of the company's standard livery.

With their 100 mph performance coupled with good reliability the GG1s were loved by crews and passengers alike. Meanwhile, most early American electric and diesel locomotives conformed to a classic streamlined outline with sloping windscreens above a rounded nose that usually incorporated a large central headlight and often a skirt beneath. This look would be exported all over the world from Egypt to Australia and Argentina, until it went out of fashion, to be replaced by the ubiquitous single-cab unit with rectangular 'bonnet'.

Raymond Loewy did not have a monopoly on American streamliners. The New York Central RR's J-3a Hudson Mercury of 1938 was designed by Henry Dreyfuss, also responsible for the classic American Bell telephone of 1933. The J3-a operated the famous Twentieth Century Limited between New York and Chicago. The locomotive was more

This Kansas City Southern, Louisiana & Arkansas diesel locomotive built by the Electro Motive Corporation typifies mid-twentieth century streamlined American diesel locomotives. (ETH Zürich)

Looking like something from *Flash Gordon*, the New York Central's magnificent J-3a 4-6-4s were designed by Henry Dreyfuss. (ETH Zürich)

conventional than Loewy's duplexes on the Pennsylvania, but Dreyfuss' front-end treatment was very striking, with a bullet-nosed smokebox and a curved skirt beneath. Most notably, the hemispherical front was bisected by a vertical fin with a central headlight, looking like something from contemporary comic strip *Flash Gordon*.

The J-3a was not the only American streamliner that was redolent of comic-book sci-fi imagery. There was a definite air of menace to the appearance of the Union Pacific Railroad's *City of Salina* diesel, with its futuristic headlight on the driver's cab, which itself sits above a huge bulbous nose grille. It claimed to be the first streamliner to operate on a major US railroad and its 1934 debut was greeted by a blaze of publicity.

Other notable American streamliners include the Chicago & North Western Railroad Class E4, introduced from 1938 on the mile-a-minute Chicago–Minneapolis service in direct competition with the aforementioned Hiawatha on the Milwaukee Railroad. The streamlined cladding on the E4s featured a sloping shroud at the front, and a striking livery of green with yellow speed lines.

Contemporary with the E4s, the New York, New Haven & Hartford Railroad employed a different approach to streamlining on its Baldwin Class I-5s. Instead of the front shroud and smooth sides, these modern-looking machines featured bullet-shaped boilers and a single, broad speed stripe with a pleasing reverse curve on the cab sides. They were built to hustle 800-ton passenger trains along a steeply graded route with frequent stops,

This is the futuristic, and rather menacing-looking *City of Salina* streamlined diesel set operated by the Union Pacific Railroad. (Alon Siton collection)

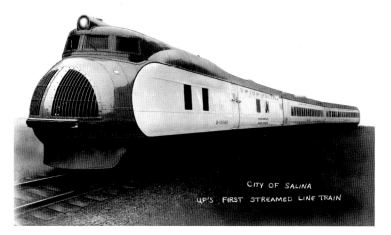

Resembling an elongated Hiawatha Atlantic, this is one of the Chicago & North Western Railroad's 4-6-4s, No. 4002. (ETH Zürich)

Compare the all-over skirt of No. 4002 above with the bullet-shaped boiler of New York, New Haven & Hartford Railroad No. 1400. She carries a bold speed stripe with a reverse curve, echoing the 'whitewall' tyres of her driving wheels. (ETH Zürich)

Displayed in Ottawa's Science and Technology Museum is Canadian National Railways' 1936-built streamlined 4-8-4 No. 6400. (Martin Cirino)

which required good acceleration. They were very reliable and popular machines but their potential was never fully realised due to the line's speed limits.

Streamlining was less widespread on the rails of Canada than was the case south of the 49th parallel. In the case of Canadian National Railways' No. 6400, the purpose of the streamlining was not to improve performance but to clear drifting smoke to improve the crew's visibility. This was once again achieved through wind tunnel testing and five 6400 series locomotives were built in Montreal in 1936. Their appearance made them an important marketing tool for CNR, and No. 6400 was chosen to haul the Royal Train in 1939. In the same year, she also appeared at that great exposition of all things streamlined, the New York World's Fair.

Streamlined locomotives were also to be seen beyond North America and Europe. Railway companies in, for example, India and Australia could see the benefit of publicity to be gained from such glamorous engines pulling their most prestigious trains. India's WP Class locomotives were of beautiful proportions and many were adorned with silver star designs on the centre of their hemispherical smokebox doors. Over 700 were built after the Second World War, and they were capable of almost 70 mph on low-grade coal.

Australia's first streamliner was South Australian Railways' No. 620, with a strikingly futuristic finned headlight on top of a large front grille and sloping speed lines along her flanks.

Even the railways of Iraq were graced by a class of locomotives whose appearance was clearly influenced by Gresley's A4s and Stanier's Coronations, and they bear more than

The line speeds permitted on India's railways meant that the streamlining applied to the WP Class Pacifics was only ever an aesthetic exercise. However, they were handsome engines and many carried beautiful decorative adornments such as stars on their smokebox doors. This is Baldwin-built No. 7203 of 1947. (Alon Siton collection)

South Australian Railways No. 620 *Sir Winston Dugan* was decorated in a livery of green and silver for the Centenary Train, which toured the state to commemorate the 100th anniversary of South Australia in 1936. (Alon Siton collection)

a passing resemblance to Doncaster's finest, especially in the profile of the valance over the wheels. Four streamliners were ordered in 1940 from Robert Stephenson & Hawthorn in Darlington. They were intended for express trains between Baghdad and Istanbul, although one was lost at sea en route from England to Iraq.

Despite the fact, for the reasons mentioned earlier, that streamlining has less of an effect on the railway than it does on the road, the more glamorous post-war trains, especially in the USA and Europe, continued to bear the hallmarks of the pre-war streamliners. The beautiful Italian Settebello and the British Blue Pullman come to mind. All modern-day high-speed trains, from the Japanese Shinkansen to the French TGV and cross-channel Eurostar, employ cutting-edge aerodynamic technology. It is ironic, then, that the world speed record was held for many years by two French electric locomotives in the 1950s that were basically rectangular boxes!

Looking like a cross between the thoroughbreds of Gresley and Stanier, this is one of the three streamlined Pacifics to make it safely to Iraq from Robert Stephenson & Hawthorns. The fourth was lost at sea. (Alon Siton collection)

This fantastic colour photograph, taken in May 1953, shows two streamlined diesel trains built in Germany by Linke Hofmann Busch. On the left, with more than a passing resemblance to the pre-war Fliegender Hamburger, is an articulated set for the Ferrocarril del Sur Este in Mexico. Beside it, and borrowing more aesthetically from the age of jet aircraft, is the Deutsche Bundesbahn's Senator. This was exhibited at the German Transport Exhibition of 1953, but was beset by mechanical failures. (Alon Siton collection)

4

Streamlining in the Air

A 1943 publication by US firm DuPont, *Glimpses into the Wonder World of Tomorrow*, predicted that after the Second World War, there would be a huge demand for streamlined personal aircraft, including teardrop-shaped helicopters, rendering the motor car a thing of the past. An illustration therein shows a shop assistant being asked to put a shopper's groceries into her blue helicopter parked outside. Thankfully, this has yet to happen, but there was still a clamour for the glamour of streamlining.

Pioneering German aviator Otto Lilienthal said 'It is easy to invent a flying machine; more difficult to build one; to make it fly is everything.' Lilienthal is described as the first true aviator. His series of experimental gliders made him world famous and demonstrated the potential for manned flight. Using a mechanical whirling arm, he calculated, erroneously as it happened, that the use of flat aerofoils would make this a reality.

Meanwhile Sir Hiram Maxim, the American inventor of the portable machine gun, was trying a different approach to manned flight, using steam power. He also trialled aerofoils using a whirling arm but moved on to wind tunnel testing. He found that a cambered profile to the aerofoil produced the best ratio of lift versus drag. His steam-powered flyer with cambered aerofoils and giant propellers was tested on a track to which it was tethered to prevent it taking off. His wings generated so much lift that it tore itself apart! Such was the early science of aerodynamics!

Famously it would be Wilbur and Orville Wright, bicycle manufacturers, who would continue the work of Lilienthal and Maxim, trying out different profiles and angles of aerofoils and assessing lift against drag, at first simply using natural wind acting on a home-made aerodynamic balance, effectively a 'wind tunnel without walls'. Through these tests they proved that the existing, accepted conventions of aerodynamic design were wrong.

They devised further tests using an ingenious test rig consisting of a bike with a third wheel rotating on a vertical axis. The aerofoils to be tested were attached to this contraption as it was ridden furiously through the streets. Realising that they needed more accurate, scientific data, they then built their own wind tunnel, followed by a second, larger version. It was in this that the Wrights were able to develop a specification for the world's first manned, powered aeroplane.

THE FIRST FLIGHT

From a 60-foot wooden track, laid on these sands Orville Wright rose into the wind on the morning of December 17, 1903. It was the first time in history that "a machine carrying a man had raised itself by its own power into the air in full flight, had sailed forward without reduction of speed, and had finally landed at a point as high as that from which it started." The flight lasted about twelve seconds.

This simple plaque at Kitty Hawk, North Carolina, for many years marked the spot where a world-changing event took place in 1903. Today, a spectacular sculpture of the aircraft and the Wright brothers themselves takes pride of place. (ETH Zürich)

How it all began. This is a working replica of the Wright Flyer IIIA, seen at Volkel in the Netherlands in 2009. (Rob de Jong)

It was at Kitty Hawk, North Carolina where, following successful tests in 1902 of a full-size glider, that Orville Wright took to the air in December 1903 in the 12 hp Wright Flyer, culminating in a flight of almost half a mile. This machine could not be considered streamlined as such, but it is included here as it represents an important milestone in the science of aerodynamics, not least the Wright brothers' contribution to the development of the wind tunnel.

It would be some decades before the science of streamlining would make an aerodynamic impact on the aeroplane, but meanwhile, a different kind of streamliner was about to take to the skies.

Balloons had been around for some time before the German Count von Zeppelin flew his first successful rigid, dirigible (meaning steerable) airship in 1906. These airborne, torpedo-shaped monsters rapidly developed into bombers, used to devastating effect on Great Britain during the First World War. By the 1920s, thanks to designers like Paul Jaray, the Zeppelin had developed into a luxury passenger-carrying airship capable of Transatlantic voyages, and its aerodynamic shape meant it could compete with the great ocean liners for speed, although carrying only a tiny fraction of the number of passengers.

At this time, the British Empire was at its maximum geographical extent, and Great Britain needed aircraft to maintain communication with its furthest reaches relatively

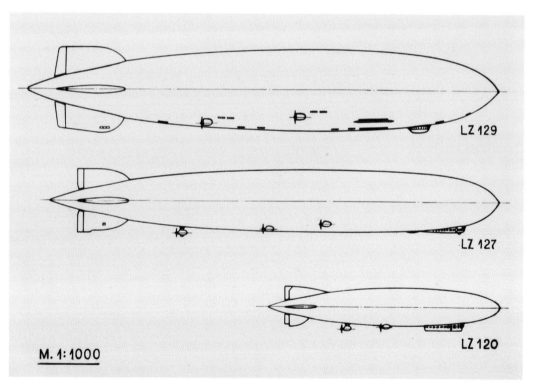

Years before he became known for the streamlining of automobiles, Paul Jaray had been responsible for developing the curving, tapered shape of post-First World War Zeppelin airships. This replaced the parallel, cylindrical profile of the wartime military craft. This drawing also shows how the ships increased in size. (ETH Zürich)

Friedrichshafen in Southern Germany is now home to the Zeppelin Museum, and was the place where these airborne monsters were built. This is LZ126 *USS Los Angeles*, over the Zeppelin airfield. Her scale can be appreciated by the size of the figures on the ground. (ETH Zürich)

quickly. In 1921 it was decided to construct two airships. They became known as the R100, built by Charles Burney's Airship Guarantee Company in Yorkshire and designed by Barnes Wallis of dam-busting bouncing bomb fame, and the Air Ministry's R101. Both shared the same elongated, pointed elliptical shape. Tragedy befell the R101 in 1930, and the German Zeppelin *Hindenberg* seven years later, with major loss of life in both cases, and the glamorous days of airship travel were over.

By this time, the fixed-wing aircraft had evolved from the boxy, angular biplanes of the First World War into something far more graceful. The maximum speed of a typical First World War fighter plane was little more than 100 mph. If higher speeds were to be achieved, the science of aerodynamics was needed. Of course, since the days of Lilienthal, Maxim and the Wright brothers, aviators had applied aerodynamic principles to the design of aerofoils (wings), but now a more holistic approach was needed, transforming the entire aircraft, and principally the fuselage, into something that slipped through the air with the greatest of ease.

Reckoned by some to be the first example of a streamlined, fixed-wing aeroplane, the Deperdussin Monocoque was designed by Louis Béchéreau and Frederick Koolhoven. Its pioneering use of a streamlined, stressed-skin shell structure would eventually become an international design standard. This pretty little machine first flew in 1911, a refined evolutionary step from Louis Blériot's English Channel-crossing monoplane. The design

It was quickly apparent that the development of fixed-wing aircraft was the way to go, and airships would disappear. The pretty little Deperdussin Monocoque of 1911 led the way in terms of aerodynamics. This one resides in the French Air and Space Museum at Le Bourget, near Paris. (Alexis Gracia)

of the aeroplane had already come a long way in less than a decade since the Wrights' maiden flight at Kitty Hawk, and the Deperdussin was a decade ahead of her time. In 1912, a Monocoque made history in Chicago's Gordon-Bennett Trophy Race, becoming the first aeroplane to break the 100 mph barrier.

Another early exponent of streamlining in the air was the Vickers Vimy Commercial, one of the first airliners, developed from the twin-engined biplane bomber of 1917, in one of which Alcock and Brown made the first non-stop flight across the Atlantic Ocean. The transition from bomber to passenger plane necessitated a fuselage of much larger cross-section, so a bulbous nose cone was added to reduce drag.

A far more important milestone in the history of aviation aerodynamics was the appearance of the incredibly innovative Junkers J-13 of 1919. In the design of this little machine, Hugo Junkers reinvented the aeroplane. Historian Charles Gibbs-Smith wrote that it was 'the first practical cantilever-wing aeroplane, the first practical all-metal aeroplane, and the first low-wing monoplane.' The mass-produced version was known as the F-13, and featured a low wing, enclosed cabin and a high degree of streamlining. The fluted aluminium structure would reappear in the later, larger JU-52. The F-13 marked the

Above: The bulbous
nose cone of the
Vickers Vimy
Commercial was
intended to reduce
the aerodynamic drag
presented by her broad
fuselage. (ETH Zürich)

Left: The appearance
of the highly advanced
Junkers F-13 of 1919
marked the reinvention
of the aeroplane.
(ETH Zürich)

beginning of global aviation and of quantity production of aircraft, and put Germany at the forefront of this transport revolution.

While Junkers was riding the crest of the German aviation industry wave, one Adolf Rohrbach narrowly missed out on rivalling him. The engineering of Rohrbach's aircraft was fundamentally different to that favoured by Junkers. Whereas the J-13/F-13 and later JU-52 relied on a framework with a corrugated skin, Rohrbach used stressed-skin duralumin construction. His Zeppelin-Staaken E4/20 of 1920 was a graceful, streamlined, four-engined aircraft with capacity for eighteen passengers, and was highly advanced for 1920 when compared with, for example, the near-contemporary Vimy. Sadly, the manufacturing restrictions placed on Germany following the 1918 Armistice meant that the prototype had to be destroyed. Many of Rohrbach's features, however, such as the overall arrangement and proportions of the aircraft, its beautiful tapered wings and stressed-skin duralumin construction would become standard in large aircraft of the future.

Rohrbach's graceful, futuristic duralumin E4/20 of 1920. (ETH Zürich)

The Caudron C.81 was a definite advance on the Vimy, but, being a biplane, was a retrograde step compared to Rohrbach's E4/20. (ETH Zürich)

The French Caudron C.81 was a three-engined biplane airliner introduced in 1923. Its fuselage was more elegant than the Vimy, perhaps influenced by Rohrbach's E4/20, with a shark-like profile and streamlined fairings over the wing-mounted engines.

Another landmark in the evolution of airborne streamlining was the appearance of the Lockheed Vega in 1927. Engineered by Jack Northrop and Jerry Vultee, whose creation is described by John Magoffin, owner of the only Vega still airworthy, as 'a revolution in the sky'. It was in one of these that Amelia Earhart became the first woman to fly solo across the Atlantic, crossing from Newfoundland to Northern Ireland, in 1932. Less well known is that, by then, Wiley Post and Harold Gatty had set off in their Vega on the first circumnavigation around the world in a fixed-wing aircraft. The little Lockheed was designed as a transport plane but was faster than contemporary American fighter aircraft. Earhart's example was finished in a striking red livery with gold speed lines and stylish valances over the undercarriage.

The beautifully streamlined Dewoitine D-27, introduced in 1928, was a fighter with an aerodynamically refined fuselage, on which even the wheel struts look like knife edges for cutting through the air. The sizes of the relatively small wing and tail area were calculated during testing in the Laboratoire Eiffel wind tunnel.

A much larger aircraft was the German Junkers JU-52 trimotor, of which thousands were built from 1930. If we look beyond the prominent engine cowlings, it can be seen that the remainder of the aeroplane is of a very rakish, angular and streamlined shape. This, together with its innovative use of lightweight corrugated duralumin alloy, helped it to its top speed of over 160 mph, a 60 mph improvement over the Vimy and the C.81. It could also carry more than twice as many passengers as these earlier airliners. A military version saw extensive use in the Second World War, and one was used as Hitler's personal transport.

This is the Lockheed Vega in which Amelia Earhart flew across the Atlantic. The little red aeroplane is in the Smithsonian Museum in Washington DC. (Victoria Pickering)

Above: By 1928, when the Dewoitine D-27 took to the air, the need for streamlining of aircraft was universally understood. (ETH Zürich)

Below left and below right: Sharing the same fluted duralumin construction as its smaller ancestor, the F-13, this is the JU-52 trimotor. The combination of lightweight materials and aerodynamic efficiency meant the aircraft was able to carry bigger loads faster than earlier transport planes. (ETH Zürich)

Reginald Mitchell, designer of the iconic Supermarine Spitfire, appreciated the importance of streamlining, as evidenced by the victory of his S6B seaplane in the 1931 Schneider Trophy. In doing so it became the fastest machine in the world, topping 400 mph. His streamlining even extended to consideration of how to cool the engine without adversely affecting the aerodynamics, with the coolant flowing between the double skins of the aircraft's floats and wings. He also employed the novel technique of flush riveting, resulting in smooth surfaces to slip through the air.

1931 also saw the debut of the Lockheed 9B Orion, a development of the Vega. The little Lockheed could reach almost 200 mph, rivalling contemporary fighters for speed. When Swissair took delivery of the American plane in 1931, it prompted other European airlines to respond. The German airline Lufthansa did so when it specified a faster, larger airliner, and both Junkers and Heinkel were challenged to meet this specification. It was

Reginald Mitchell's 400 mph Supermarine S6B seaplane. This one was exhibited at the 1951 Festival of Britain. (John Alexander, MBE)

It was the performance of the Lockheed 9B Orion that prompted German aircraft manufacturers to raise their game. This example was operated by Swissair and was photographed in the entrance to a hangar at Dübendorf airfield in Switzerland. (ETH Zürich)

the performance of the Orion that prompted German manufacturer Heinkel to launch its He70 Blitz, a high-speed four-passenger aircraft with a beautiful, streamlined fuselage.

Heinkel's new aircraft featured elliptical wings, differing from those on Mitchell's Spitfire by virtue of the angled, inverted 'gull-wing' bend in them. The transition between fuselage and wing was smoothly radiused. Much of the Heinkel's aerodynamic shape was based upon a 1925-built racing aircraft built by Paul Bäumer, First World War ace fighter pilot, dentist, and aircraft manufacturer. His streamlined, two-seater *Sausewind* ('rushing wind') is really the definitive prototype for the streamlined prop-driven aircraft. It was designed by brothers Siegfried and Walter Gunter, with beautiful, sweeping elliptical wings and tail on a smooth monocoque fuselage.

When these refinements were incorporated into the design of the new Heinkel, it delivered even better performance than anticipated, enabling a maximum of 234 mph. A later version, equipped in Britain with a Rolls-Royce engine reached 298 mph.

The Blitz evolved into the He70E light bomber and reconnaissance plane for the Luftwaffe but the elliptical wings proved to be its flaw and it was not a success in military use.

The wing shape, along with some of the other aerodynamic features of the He70, influenced the design of the much larger He111, the most important German medium bomber of the Second World War. It was designed by the Gunther brothers, who used the He70 as their starting point, in particular its streamlined features. Every surface of the new, much larger aircraft was rounded for maximum aerodynamic efficiency. Less well known than the bomber variant was the elegant He111C airliner of 1936, whose fuselage was, if anything, even more streamlined than its military counterpart.

The Heinkel He111 bomber was one of the deadliest weapons of the Second World War. Less well known was its civilian equivalent, the He111C airliner. This one, in the colours of Lufthansa, is on the ground at Dübendorf. (ETH Zürich)

1933 was a big year in aeronautical history, for it marked the debut of two aeroplanes that would completely revolutionise commercial air transport. They were the Boeing 247 and the Douglas DC-1. First to appear was the Boeing, with its slender, low-mounted cantilevered wings, vee-shaped cockpit windscreens, smooth all-metal construction and retractable landing gear. These features, combined with powerful, supercharged engines, gave the 247 a top speed 50 percent higher than any rival.

Meanwhile the Douglas Aircraft Corporation had charged two of its designers, Arthur Raymond and James 'Dutch' Kindelberger, with designing an airliner capable of beating the Boeing. Their DC-1 made its debut a few months after the 247. The two rival machines had much in common in terms of engineering, and both were designed to remain airborne if one of their two engines failed. This ability was no doubt aided by their wind-tunnel tested aerodynamics. The solitary DC-1 prototype led to the production series DC-2, which had a slightly elongated fuselage. In January 1935, *Scientific American* magazine said, 'There is not the slightest doubt that American airliners now surpass the designs of every other country. Without prejudice to the other fine ships, the Douglas DC-2 may be recorded as the supreme American achievement in transport design.' It set speed records and rendered the 247 obsolete in one fell swoop, less than two years after the Boeing's launch. The Douglas was quieter, faster and more spacious inside. It also ushered in the era of the in-flight movie.

The legendary DC-3 would follow soon after. Douglas' Chief Power Plant Engineer Ivar Shogran once said, 'We made the DC-3 without a computer to test it. There was plenty of data from the DC-1 and DC-2 to formulate the design. Often we got down on the floor and worked things out ourselves. There was personal ingenuity, and application, and we made things happen overnight.'

The swift Boeing 247 of 1933 was the first true modern airliner. This example was captured over the County Wicklow countryside south of Dublin, on its way to preservation in the Science Museum's storage facility at Wroughton, near Swindon. (Malcolm Nason)

Another spectacular mid-air shot showing a Swiss Air Lines Douglas DC-2 over the wintry shores of Lake Zürich. (ETH Zürich)

Swiss Air must have been impressed with the DC-2, for it also took delivery of a fleet of DC-3s. This one was photographed at Zürich's Kloten Airport. (ETH Zürich)

The DC-3 was designed to meet a specification from American Airlines for a sleeper airliner for overnight flights. The DC-2 was used as a basis, and the fuselage was widened to accommodate sleeping berths. More powerful engines were needed for the new, larger aircraft, which was effectively the first wide-bodied airliner.

Ergonomic considerations came into play, with designers Bill Littlewood and Harry Wetzel trying out mock ups of sleeping berths for size, and testing different positions for reading lights and hostess call buttons. Ideas to improve passenger comfort were borrowed from the Pullman Car Company, a name synonymous with luxury rail travel.

What emerged in December 1935 was a completely new aeroplane, more powerful and larger in every respect than its DC-2 progenitor.

In June 1936, American Airlines' DC-3 Flagship service between Newark, New Jersey, and Chicago began. Just as the DC-2 introduced movies on board, the DC-3 was the first American airliner to offer hot meals, an innovation pioneered in Germany in the 1920s. Over 10,000 DC-3s were built and the C-47 military derivative would become a Second World War icon.

Arthur Raymond said, 'We didn't know we were building a legend', and the entire aviation industry praised the DC-3. Incredibly, by 1939, 90 percent of the world's air traffic was being carried by DC-3s. The pioneering, beautifully streamlined Douglas Commercials had laid the foundations for all future airliners.

Following the global success of the DC-3, the American aeronautical industry would dominate the airline markets of the western world, although ironically it would be Boeing that would triumph in the end, and not Douglas.

Britain's De Havilland Dragon Rapide was much smaller than the American airliners we have just seen, and was a throwback to the days of the biplane. Her streamlined fuselage and engine cowlings make her a thing of beauty. This example carries RAF markings and is used for pleasure flights under the brand name 'Classic Wings' from Duxford in Cambridgeshire. (Colin Alexander)

In Britain, the pretty little De Havilland Dragon Rapide of 1934 was a slightly anachronistic streamliner, for her aerodynamic, modern fuselage and smooth engine cowlings with integral undercarriage fairings were carried on biplane wings. Two other notable streamlined De Havillands that bravely tried to stave off American competition were the DH91 Albatross and the post-war Comet, which was the world's first jet airliner but which was fatally flawed. The DH91 of 1938 was described as the most beautiful four-propeller airliner ever to fly.

The DH91 met an Air Ministry specification for a long-distance mail carrier and passenger airliner. For its designer, Arthur Hagg, aerodynamics was a major factor, resulting in a beautifully smooth fuselage and minimal air resistance on leading edges. The wings were based on those used on DH88 Comet Racer, which saw off competition from both a Boeing 247 and a Douglas DC-2 to win the 1934 MacRobertson Air Race from London to Melbourne, beating both by around twenty hours. The Albatross had a monocoque fuselage of flexible plywood and balsa, a technique famously used on the De Havilland Mosquito of the Second World War.

Mention of the Mosquito leads us nicely to what the author considers the most beautiful aeroplane of all time, the Supermarine Spitfire, whose origins can be traced back to her designer, Reginald Mitchell's aforementioned S6B Schneider Trophy seaplane. While it is true that the slightly earlier Hawker Hurricane was more numerous, and was responsible for more 'kills' against the Luftwaffe, only the slippery Spitfire could match the German Messerschmitt 109 for speed. The outline of Mitchell's fighter was a symphony of sweeping curves and its elliptical wings made it an instantly recognisable design icon. The Spitfire's shape was influenced by the Heinkel He70 and therefore, by default, Bäumer's *Sausewind* of 1925. Beverly Shenstone, who was responsible for the fighter's aerodynamic design, praised the German aircraft, acknowledging the fact that they had flown with the perfect elliptical wing shape a full decade earlier.

Only four years after the Dragon Rapide appeared, De Havilland introduced the modern-looking DH91 Albatross. Imperial Airways' G-AFDJ was photographed on the ground at Dübendorf in Switzerland. (ETH Zürich)

Reginald Mitchell's masterpiece, the sleek, handsome Supermarine Spitfire, was one of the aircraft that helped the Allies to victory in the Second World War. This restored example is at the wonderful Eden Camp Museum in North Yorkshire. (Colin Alexander)

The Lockheed Constellation was designed to 'carry more people farther and faster than ever before, and economically enough to broaden the acceptance of flying as an alternative to train, ship and automobile'. The distinctive sweeping curves of the fuselage and triple tailplane can be seen on this preserved 'Connie' in Tucson, Arizona. (Stewart Robotham)

Speaking of sweeping curves, an ambitious 1939 design brief outlined by Howard Hughes and accepted by Lockheed would result in a revolutionary aircraft that was capable of America's first coast-to-coast, non-stop service. This was the Lockheed Constellation. Chief research engineer Kelly Johnson stated that it would 'carry more people farther and faster than ever before, and economically enough to broaden the acceptance of flying as an alternative to train, ship and automobile.' And it would achieve all of this in a beautiful, streamlined, dolphin-like fuselage, putting Lockheed, and its customer Trans World Airlines, firmly on the aviation map.

The Constellation was flown by airlines and military bodies all over the world for decades, and was one of the most graceful propeller-driven airliners. It was faster than most Second World War fighters, being capable of 350 mph. It carried forty-four passengers in its pressurised cabin, technology pioneered by Lockheed, permitting the aircraft to fly above most turbulence, resulting in smoother travel.

Like most of her contemporaries, she was equally beautiful in both form and function. Howard Hughes himself publicised the new airliner in inimitable style, breaking the transcontinental speed record from California to Washington, D.C., averaging 331 mph, and crossing America in just under seven hours. Rather poignantly, during military testing of the Constellation at Wright Field, Ohio, one of the co-pilots was none other than Orville Wright, making his last ever flight before hanging up his flying jacket.

Of course, in the years to follow, generations of increasingly aerodynamic aircraft would enter service, reaching speeds undreamed of by the Wright brothers, allowing the human race to break the sound barrier and even leave the Earth's atmosphere altogether.

Typical of post-war commercial airliners, embodying the lessons in streamlining learned through decades of practice, was the Vickers Vanguard of 1960, one of which is seen at Heathrow in the colours of British European Airways. (John Alexander, MBE)

5

Streamlining on the Waves

Although chronologically, Sir Charles Parsons' *Turbinia* preceded almost every machine mentioned so far, being launched in 1894, she has a place here because Parsons' holistic approach to streamlining made her by far the fastest ship at the time. As mentioned earlier, she combined the most slender hydrodynamic hull, eleven times longer than she was broad, with the most advanced screws (propellors) and Parsons' latest steam turbine.

His turbines, which were of course meticulously streamlined internally, would go on to power much of the Royal Navy and great liners such as the *Mauretania*, which held the Transatlantic Blue Riband speed record for twenty years.

P-551 M.F. Kalakala

The extraordinary MV *Kalakala*, designed by Boeing, crossing Puget Sound, Washington. (Hank Zaletel)

The world's first truly streamlined commercial ship, stylistically, was rather surprisingly not a glamorous ocean liner but a ferry for the Puget Sound Navigation Company in Seattle, Washington. The MV *Kalakala* entered service in 1935, a year after the Chrysler Airflow hit the road. She was designed by none other than Boeing to the order of Captain Alexander Peabody, president of the PSNC, who wanted a new flagship unlike anything seen before. She was intended as a symbol of hope, a welcome distraction from the bleak reality of the Depression, offering dances and social cruises as well as regular ferry traffic.

Her superstructure used no rivets, the completely smooth surfaces being achieved by electro-welding. Curves abounded everywhere, from her outsize portholes to the benches on the passenger decks. Her bridge was set back from her streamlined superstructure for aesthetic reasons, making it impossible to see her bow from the helm. Although not an entire success story, the *Kalakala* is certainly worthy of a place in any chapter about streamlined vessels.

Back on the oceans, the RMS *Queen Mary* of 1936 was one of the most iconic liners ever built, a floating art deco palace powered by Parsons' latest steam turbines. Some of her styling reflected the public appetite for streamlining, but not as much as her glamorous French rival and contemporary. The SS *Normandie* was graced with beautiful white-painted curves sweeping up from her foredeck, and this fashion would continue into the streamlined modernism of the liners of the 1950s. Of course, the difference made

The graceful curves of the SS *Normandie*, whose opulent art deco interior epitomised the glamour of ocean liner travel between the wars. (Colin Alexander collection)

by streamlining the superstructure of a ship to her performance when travelling at 10–30 knots would be negligible, whether on Puget Sound or the Atlantic.

There have, however, been examples of boats on which streamlining definitely made a difference, and so we return to the quest for speed. Not content with just the land speed record, Malcolm Campbell also pursued the maximum speed on water. His *Bluebird K4* jet-propelled boat set a new world water speed record of 142 mph on Coniston Water, in the Lake District, in 1939. He had already broken the record three times in her predecessor, *K3*, a conventional 'planing' powerboat with a single keel. At high speed, the force of the onrushing water against the keel lifts the bow, reducing the amount of surface area in contact with the water and reducing frictional drag.

The more advanced *K4* was a hydroplane with three points of contact with the water, two at the bow and the third at the stern. As speed increases the hull lifts clear of the water and the boat planes on those three contact points, causing much less drag. This reduction in drag comes with a price, however, for if the bow of the craft lifts beyond its safety margin, the aerodynamic force (not the hydrodynamic force of the water) on the airborne hull causes it to flip. This, tragically, is what happened to *Bluebird K7* in 1967, when Michael Campbell's son, Donald, was killed on Coniston at over 300 mph.

A full-size replica of Malcolm Campbell's *Bluebird K4* in the Lakeland Motor Museum, Cumbria. (Colin Alexander)

It could be said that Campbell paid with his life for the discovery that there is a limit to what can be achieved with streamlining on water. Indeed the record still stands at 318 mph, not much faster than that achieved by *Bluebird*, and has been held since 1978 by Australian Ken Warby in his *Spirit of Australia*.

The streamlined aesthetic of the stateliest liners and most glamorous cruise ships lasted well into the 1960s with the *Queen Elizabeth II*. One of the most graceful examples was the SS *Northern Star* of the Shaw Savill and Albion Line. She was built by Vickers Armstrong in Newcastle and powered by Parsons turbines. Her underwater profile was the result of exhaustive hydrodynamic tests, and above the waterline she had a flared bow and streamlined superstructure and funnel. The vertical emphasis of her predecessor, the *Dominion Monarch*, was replaced by curves and rakish angles. Inside, her furnishing and decor were minimalist and modern.

All of this is in contrast to the liners and cruise ships of today, some of which resemble floating tower blocks, and many of which have lost the glamour and style that was the hallmark of ocean travel.

Alongside *K4* is a replica of Donald Campbell's *Bluebird K7*. (Colin Alexander)

6

Stationary Streamlining

Brendan Cormier, curator of *Cars: Accelerating The Modern World*, said 'Of course, that a scientific study of aerodynamics ... would be translated to a world of static objects that were hardly in need of going anywhere fast is one of the great comedies of twentieth-century design.'

It is easy to deride the efforts of 1930s designers to 'streamline' fridges and telephones as gimmickry, but we must not forget that products will always bear the visual hallmarks of whatever is the current trend. In addition, the fact that streamlining could be seen as scientific and efficient gave it serious justification over other passing trends. Seeing the public-relations effect of streamlined cars and trains, manufacturers turned their designers to styling all manner of mundane objects with sleek curves and tapers, anything that would symbolise the modern, efficient world and a bright future. There was a practical reason too, for in many cases the combination of smoother shapes and new materials and manufacturing methods made quantity production of streamlined products more cost-effective than the products they replaced.

It was in 1930s America that product designers began taking the streamlining motifs from the world of transport, transforming static objects. The futuristic look of films like Fritz Lang's *Metropolis* captured the public imagination and manufacturers were quick to tap into this fashion to increase sales.

It was usually through the purchase of relatively small objects that consumers were first exposed to the art of streamlining. Ronson became known for its streamlined cigarette lighters from the 1920s onwards, using the latest plastics combined with chrome-plating. That company's use of streamlined forms continued right through to the 1950s.

Although smoking was in those days regarded as glamorous, to modern eyes RCA's Victor Special Portable Phonograph seems a far more glamorous product than a cigarette lighter. This beautifully smooth chrome-plated record player was designed in the early 1930s by Romanian John Vassos, based in America. Vassos was well known for his televisions sets and radios that invariably carried an art deco motif, as did his iconic subway-station turnstile.

Even objects as large and cumbersome as refrigerators were given the streamline treatment. The 'fridge' had evolved from a wooden box resembling a large cupboard into

Above: A later example from a long line of streamlined Ronson cigarette lighters, this is the 1958 Futura Varaflame, housed in a streamlined boat. (Joe Haupt)

Right: The beautiful RCA Victor Special Portable Phonograph, as displayed in the Brooklyn Museum of Art. (The Kozy Shack)

a prime example of 'form following function', with an external cooling unit mounted prominently on the top of a steel box. Even though they were, at their time, the latest in kitchen technology, they were often rather incongruously, supported on 'Queen Anne' style legs. In 1934, Raymond Loewy swept away this anachronism with his Sears Roebuck Coldspot Super 6 refrigerator, and previously, Henry Dreyfuss had made the cooling unit integral with the box. Loewy's design used many elements of streamlining, such as the subtle curves and the bold chevron-like ribs pressed into the door, transforming the fridge into an object of desire. The modern kitchen appliance was born and the age of consumerism had arrived, bringing with it the concept of built-in obsolescence. New, 'must-have' models appeared constantly, vying for the attention of a public eager to raise their status among neighbours by showing off the latest streamlined products.

When Charlotte Perriand applied for a job with the great architect Le Corbusier she was rejected, being told 'we don't sew cushions here'. He had to rethink his decision when he saw a popular exhibition of her furniture designs at the Paris Autumn Salon of 1927. She went on to design, among other things, a beautiful, modern chaise longue capable of rocking in its cradle. Its legs mimic aeroplane wings and with its curved, linear shape, it sits comfortably in the streamlined genre of its day.

Perriand was not the only notable female designer of the era. One whose work was envied by Le Corbusier was Irishwoman Eileen Gray, who was fifty-one years old when she tackled her first essay in architecture in 1929. This was Villa E1027 in Saint-Tropez on the Côte d'Azur. It was full of new ideas and she described it as 'a dwelling as a living organism'. It was

American streamlined refrigerators. On the left is a Kelvinator and on the right is a Loewy-designed Sears Roebuck Coldspot, in the Anderson-Beardsley House in Tecumseh, Michigan. I am not sure what Raymond Loewy would have thought of the pink paint job applied by the owner. (Stephen Brown)

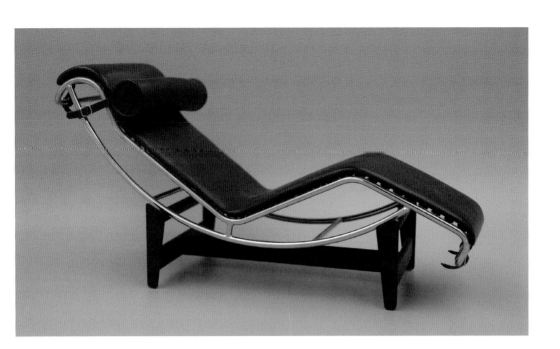

Above: Although this is a 1:6 scale model, it shows clearly the modern, streamlined profile of Charlotte Perriand's chaise longue of 1927. (Michele Brown)

Right: Eileen Gray's streamlined, functional, height-adjustable E1027 table. (Flying Puffin)

furnished with her own designs, some of them custom-made for this house. They included the streamlined yet functional, height-adjustable E1027 table. Made of stainless steel and glass, it is acknowledged as a collectable twentieth-century design icon.

Radios were a focal point in most homes of the era and many borrowed aesthetic references from streamlined cars and aircraft. A perfect example is the wonderful late 1930s Czechoslovakian Tesla Talisman radio with its Bakelite casing in an imaginatively styled, sweeping asymmetric shape that looks wind-tunnel tested.

The Petipoint Flat Iron of 1937 was an exuberant example of product design incorporating streamlined motifs. Its designer was the multitalented Clifford Brooks Stevens, of Western Flyer motor home and Hiawatha lounge car fame. For this brief he was aided by Edward P. Schreyer. The iron's stylish cooling wings were borrowed from aeronautical practice and its rakishly angled handle suggests speed.

Although perhaps the Bakelite casing has not aged well, visually, the streamlined shape and horizontal fluting on the Tesla Talisman radio are timeless. (Big Jim McBob)

Clifford Brooks Stevens was a multi-disciplinary exponent of streamline design, from motor homes to railway carriages to the Petipoint Flat Iron. This example is displayed for posterity in the David Owsley Museum of Art, at Ball State University, Muncie, Indiana. (David Ellis)

Photography for the masses was becoming an affordable reality at this time, and the boxy Kodak Brownie was an iconic, if not particularly stylish design that made it possible. Walter Dorwin Teague's compact and streamlined Kodak Bullet camera of 1936 continued that popularity, combining practicality with the latest style.

In the 1970s, Dieter Rams, the great German industrial designer, set out his ten principles for good design. He said products should be innovative, useful, aesthetic, understandable, unobtrusive, honest, long-lasting, thorough down to the last detail, environmentally friendly, and, finally, good design should be 'as little design as possible'. While some of the streamlined icons we have seen don't meet all of those principles, George Scharfenberg's beautiful Sunbeam T-9 toaster of 1939 comes very close. With its curved, streamlined style and simple etched decoration, it was an extremely popular model. The internal mechanism operated as smoothly as its

Walter Dorwin Teague's compact and streamlined Kodak Bullet camera of 1936 was a beautiful, simple and intuitive piece of industrial design. (Guy Iordat)

Not only was George Scharfenberg's elegant Sunbeam T-9 toaster a commercial success, it also followed the principles of good design, as set out by Dieter Rams. (Terry F. Luehmann)

external streamlining would suggest; no 'popping up' here, as the toast rose serenely from the slots.

At first glance, in comparison to some of these other products, the Airline chair of 1934 looks a little dated, but we must not allow the materials and colours to detract from its streamline form. The chair was designed in 1939 by Kem Weber for the Walt Disney Studios in Los Angeles, for which he was architect. The tan upholstery was chosen by Disney himself, and 300 chairs were bought by the studios. It was an early example of flat-pack furniture but it never went into mass production, Weber preferring to use an LA-based cabinetmaker.

In fact streamline styling permeated every aspect of product design. As well as the above there were juicers and vacuum cleaners, clocks and cutlery, hats and shoes that all bore the visual influence of the streamlined world around them. This aesthetic was also reflected in the graphic design that advertised the products.

Of course, for the style-conscious 1930s consumer it would never do to place the most fashionable streamline furniture in a stuffy old Victorian house. The true aficionado of the streamlined lifestyle would want the latest in streamlined housing, too, to showcase their expensive goods.

We saw Buckminster Fuller's Dymaxion car earlier. He also designed the streamlined, environmentally efficient, mass-produced Dymaxion house. He had the idea of using the capacity and techniques of the wartime aviation industry for peacetime prefabricated house construction. The Dymaxion was designed to go anywhere and was entirely self-sustaining, with no need to be connected to mains water or electricity.

Fuller designed a home that was heated and cooled by natural means, that made its own power, was earthquake and storm-proof, and made of permanent, engineered materials that required no periodic painting, reroofing, or other maintenance. The owner could easily change the floor plan as required, squeezing the bedrooms to make the living room bigger

Ignoring perhaps the tan colour scheme of the Airline chair, designed by Kem Weber for the Walt Disney Studios, we can appreciate its modern streamlined shape. (Tim Evanson)

This is, I believe, the sole-surviving complete example of Buckminster Fuller's ingenious Dymaxion house, on display at the Henry Ford Museum in Dearborn, Michigan. (Bruce Gage)

for a party, for instance. Like so many products we have seen, Fuller's Dymaxion house was simply years ahead of its time, and perhaps we have still not caught up with his genius.

Sadly, though, just like the Chrysler Airflow, the Dymaxion house did not really catch on, the American consumer preferring a more traditional home.

While the Dymaxion was truly streamlined in every sense of the word, inside and out, the architectural style known as Streamline Moderne was very much a cosmetic treatment. It often appeared on buildings associated with transport, such as bus terminals, railway stations, airports and roadside cafés. It was characterised by strong horizontal motifs including flat roofs, radiused corners, glass bricks and circular porthole windows, and the use of chrome plating.

One of the most notable examples in Britain is the Midland Hotel in Morecambe, Lancashire. It was built in 1933 to replace the original of the same name, and belonged to the London, Midland & Scottish Railway. The architect was Oliver Hill, and renowned sculptor Eric Gill was responsible for its interior decoration. It was very much 'the place to be', with clientele including Laurence Oliver, Coco Chanel and Noel Coward.

Oliver Hill and Eric Gill achieved harmony in the hotel's architecture and interior. Hill claimed that he had designed 'the first really modern hotel in the country.'

As with so many of the designs we have seen, fashionable, modern materials such as chromium and vitrolite were used. The Midland was opened in a fanfare of publicity, with

Above: The beautiful Midland Hotel at Morecambe, Lancashire. The same Eric Gill who designed its interior decor was responsible for the LNER's Gill Sans typeface. (Andrew Skinner)

Left: The innovative De La Warr Pavilion in Bexhill-on-Sea, Sussex. (Musical Photo Man)

Architecture Illustrated devoting an entire issue to Hill and Gill's masterpiece. Sir Josiah Stamp, President of the London, Midland & Scottish, compared it to the newest hotels he had seen in America and Europe and declared that the Midland 'eclipsed them all'.

An equally grand English seaside essay in Streamline Moderne is the De La Warr Pavilion in the south coast resort of Bexhill-on-Sea. At its 1935 inauguration, Herbrand Sackville, 9th Earl De La Warr, whose innovative socialist thinking later inspired the Festival of Britain and the Arts Council, described the pavilion as 'A modernist building of world renown that will become a crucible for creating a new model of cultural provision in an English seaside town which is going to lead to the growth, prosperity and the greater culture of our town.'

Not only was the De La Warr ahead of its time architecturally, its very purpose was groundbreaking. It was intended as a 'People's Palace', an experimental exercise in social democracy, the progenitor of the modern arts centre. Nothing like it had been seen before in Britain. The architects were Eric Mendelsohn and Serge Chermayeff and it was the first welded, steel-framed structure in Britain, with echoes of Bauhaus style and many elements associated with streamlining.

40 miles west of Bexhill is the port of Shoreham, and situated here is a contemporary of the De La Warr Pavilion, another stylish architectural nod towards streamlining. Shoreham's Airport Terminal was designed by R. Stavers Hessell Tiltman, probably Britain's foremost airport designer of the era. At this time, international air travel was becoming fashionable and seen as forward-thinking. Channel Air Ferries and Jersey Airways operated scheduled flights from Shoreham to various British destinations as well as Jersey and France. High-profile visitors to the new facility included legendary aviators Amy Johnson and Charles Lindbergh. The main building combines straight lines and curves in typical Streamline Moderne style, and it is a rare survivor of a pre-war airport terminal, both inside and out.

As well as its iconic streamline-style buses, the Greyhound company in the USA was equally famous for its beautiful, landmark bus terminals, which represented some of the best examples of architectural streamlining.

The man responsible for establishing this new image for Greyhound's bus stations was architect William Strudwick Arrasmith. His first new terminal opened in Louisville, Kentucky, in 1937, to coincide with the introduction of Loewy's Supercoach. Arrasmith evolved the streamline style into an architectural Greyhound corporate identity, with geometric canopies incorporating the company logo. The continuously smooth horizontals were accentuated by the use of glazing that wrapped around the radiused corners, and enamelled steel panelling in glossy blue with white lining to match the new vehicles.

Right and overleaf above: Shoreham Airport exemplifies streamline architecture inside and out, and is a precious survivor. (Clive Barker)

This visual harmony between vehicles and terminals was something quite new, but there was more to Arrasmith's work than making his buildings pretty. His treatment of the design of bus terminals was holistic. They had to work, and they were sited on pieces of land of varying shape and size. What was constant was the need for Greyhound's giant buses to swing in and out, with overhangs beyond front and rear axles and a fixed turning circle. As well as calculating the space required for the efficient movement of vehicles, Arrasmith also considered the movement of passengers inside the terminal, allocating internal space for different facilities accordingly. This was another example of streamlining both externally and internally.

Even the smaller Greyhound bus terminals were given the streamline Arrasmith treatment. This is Jackson, Tennessee. (Darren Snow)

Just as Greyhound strove to achieve a modern, corporate identity across its vehicle fleet and infrastructure, another visual transformation was happening in London.

Frank Pick was the visionary Managing Director of London Underground in the 1920s and the first Chief Executive of London Transport as a whole. Art historian Nikolaus Pevsner called him 'the greatest patron of the arts whom this century has so far produced in England, and indeed the ideal patron of our age.'

London's Underground was the world's first, and by the end of the First World War its oldest line was fifty-five years old. Pick set about modernising all aspects of the capital's transport infrastructure, and although the streamlined 'tube' train mentioned earlier was not perpetuated, streamline style was certainly evident in the architecture of the new stations designed by Charles Holden. New trains and modernised stations displayed Harry Beck's groundbreaking map, a perfect example of graphical streamlining, where extraneous detail was removed and navigation was thereby speeded up. Frank Pick also introduced the red and blue Underground roundel and the Johnston typeface that ran through everything. All of these are recognised as timeless design icons, and it is thanks to Pick, who altered the appearance of the capital city during what some have called the golden age of transport design.

Probably the building most associated with the streamline era is one that takes us back to the automotive theme, and that is New York City's iconic Chrysler Building, designed by

London's Underground is rich in design history, and not just from the streamline era. This is Eric Aumonier's dramatic sculpture of an Archer at East Finchley station aiming his arrow at the tunnel which starts here and goes all the way to the southern end of the Northern Line at Morden. Note the architectural similarities between the station building, the Midland Hotel and the De La Warr Pavilion. (Andrew Thirlby)

William Van Alen and completed in 1930. Even though in stature it was overtaken by the Empire State Building less than a year later, and by many others since, it remains the most eye-catching element of the Manhattan skyline. At street level, its exterior is horizontal and geometric, with the emphasis changing to the vertical as it narrows and rises towards its spectacular rocket-ship apex. It gleams with stainless steel, accentuating the dramatic curves and arcs of triangular windows in a joyous sunburst pattern. Decoration is bold with stylised American eagle gargoyles jutting out from its lofty corners, and, at the request of Walter P. Chrysler, there are various automotive motifs which tied in with contemporary Chrysler cars. The building typifies the bold modernism of the late 1920s when it was considered important that the newest buildings reflected the latest technology.

The dramatic arrival of streamlining in the world of design not only heralded a new visual vocabulary, it also introduced us to many new materials and novel applications for others. Like all such movements, streamlining as a fashion statement died out, partly due to the demands of the Second World War and post-war austerity. Its legacy, however, continues in the form of today's modern, fast and economical transport and our minimalistic, stylish and efficient lifestyles.

Above and left: With its sumptuous art deco foyer, and looking like it could blast off into space any minute, this is the incredible Chrysler Building in New York City. (Colin Alexander)